SOMEDAY

IS NOT
A DAY OF THE WEEK

Unlock Your Financial Potential Today

Derrek,

Great to meet you. I hope
you find a few Pearls of wisdom
in here.

(signature)

AVIVA SAPERS AND ANDREW MacDOUGALL
Sapers & Wallack, Inc.

Aviva Sapers, Andrew MacDougall/Sapers & Wallack, Inc.
www.sapers-wallack.com

Book layout ©2022 Advisors Excel, LLC

Some Day Is Not A Day Of The Week/Aviva Sapers and Andrew MacDougall — 1st Edition.

ISBN 9798861119238

"You cannot escape the responsibility of tomorrow by evading it today."
~ Abraham Lincoln

"Only put off until tomorrow that which you are willing to die and leave undone."
~ Pablo Piccasso

"It's the job that's never started that takes the longest to finish."
~ J.R. Tolkien

"Do or do not. There is no try."
~ Jedi Master Yoda

*To those who left behind a mess
because they didn't take the time to plan.*

Table of Contents

CHAPTER 1

The Importance of Planning

J ared was at a contented place in life...right up until the day everything suddenly changed.

At the age of fifty-nine, this mid-level sales manager for a prominent New England-based biotech company could see the finish line to his long working career finally coming into view. His longtime dream of retiring to a second home somewhere in the foothills of the Green Mountains—a place where he could escape the summer heat of his Boston home, enjoy the fall foliage, and have easier access to the skiing he and his wife so enjoyed—finally seemed within reach.

It was going to take some work, to be sure. His initial goal of retiring "early" at age sixty-two, when he could first begin receiving Social Security, probably wasn't going to happen, but Jared was willing to adjust. He had saved and invested whatever he could whenever he could, regularly building up to where he was now putting 5 percent of every paycheck on a pre-tax basis into his 401(k). He and his wife Jennifer talked about investing more, but that had been tough in the family's younger years when putting their two children through parochial schools. When it came time for college, the couple considered themselves fortunate that the kids didn't have Ivy League ambitions, but even four years at Boston College wasn't cheap. Their promise to "help" the kids with their college loans ended up involving more help than they'd expected, and the bills were only just now being paid off as Jared approached 60.

So, no, Jared and Jennifer's retirement savings were not all that they had hoped to have at this point in life. But there was still time, they told themselves, especially if Jen increased her hours as a part-time accountant and Jared put off his retirement just a bit longer. He still enjoyed working, mostly because he liked the people on the sales teams he managed. New members were coming on board all the time, and training them and being around their youthful energy kept Jared young. He believed he could continue working until sixty-seven, his full retirement age at which he would receive his full Social Security benefit.

Jared figured that during the next eight of what should be his highest earning years, he and Jen could build up their retirement savings that weren't yet where they needed to be. He would maximize his pre-tax 401(k) contributions, and he and Jen would be able to pay off the mortgage on the West Roxbury family home they had recently renovated.

The couple had talked about the need to see a financial advisor, one with expertise in retirement planning, but kept finding reasons to delay the visit. Jared rarely considered getting investment counseling, figuring his own instincts were good enough. He tried to stay financially informed, and his 401(k) investment choices usually produced a growing account value. Sure, he'd experienced rough times just like everyone else during the dot-com bear market of 2000-01, and again during the Great Recession of 2007-09. But his 401(k) had rebounded from those downturns and was growing nicely in the years afterward. Here in January of 2020, Jared was feeling better about where his retirement nest egg was headed.

It might be even better, he thought, after he and Jen visited the advisor whose educational seminar they'd attended. They finally scheduled their first meeting for right after they returned from a dream winter vacation.

Jared and Jen had always been avid skiers. They were regular visitors to Maine's Sunday River ski resort, and had even skied the lower portions of trails used in the Lake Placid Olympics. So, when a company vice president offered them use of his condo in Park City, Utah, the chance to ski on some slopes used in the 2002 Salt Lake City Winter Olympics was too good to pass up.

It was on a bright, crisp, perfect day at Deer Valley that Jared was hit at high speed by a snowboarder who'd taken on a steeper slope than he could handle.

Upon arriving at a trauma center, an MRI exam revealed that the impact and resulting fall caused major cervical damage to Jared's upper spine. He was left with limited use of his extremities and doctors were unsure whether he'd ever regain full use.

Jared and Jennifer's retirement dreams were about to become a nightmare. They fared somewhat better than many people facing the same life-changing event. The biotech company he worked for had disability insurance as part of its group benefits plan that would provide 60 percent of his $150,000 base pay, $90,000 annually, up to his retirement age at sixty-seven. But given that Jared typically earned a bonus that brought his total annual compensation to around $300,000, and that Jennifer added another $100,000 or so from her accounting work, the disability coverage left the family's income a long way from what they had been living on. Jen hoped to continue part-time work even as she cared for her disabled husband, but she questioned how much time, if any, she could be away from home. And while Jared clung to the belief that he could return to some kind of work someday, it was an uncertain proposition at best, and one that would not happen without an extensive period of rehabilitation.

Now there were new expenses, a lot of new expenses. Jared and Jen initially hoped to get by with in-home nursing care, but that cost ate up much of their income. The emotional toll was even more demanding. Providing continual care for her husband soon became more than Jen could handle, and the prospect of needing custodial nursing care soon became a very expensive likelihood.

Moreover, Jared's plan to improve the couple's financial outlook was now in jeopardy. Instead of saving more for retirement, he and Jen were going to have to dip into their retirement savings earlier than they expected. To make matters even worse, the economic downturn caused by the spread of the COVID-19 virus caused a sudden and substantial drop in the stock market with a resulting plunge in the value of Jared's 401(k).

Expect the Unexpected

Jared and Jennifer are a fictional couple, but the dramatic change in their life is something we hear of all too often from very real people. The effect of any life-changing event—be it a disabling accident; sudden joblessness; an illness or debilitating disease; the death of a family's principal provider—can be especially difficult for those who've failed to plan for the unexpected.

At Sapers & Wallack, Inc, an employee benefits and financial services firm in Newton, Massachusetts, we work every day to help people prepare not only for the predictable future, but also for unpredictable scenarios like those of Jared and Jennifer.

Planning is the key when our challenge is to be ready for whatever life throws at us. We consequently plan and prepare for the times we hope never come to pass, and for that you can never do too much planning. This is why we talk with clients of all ages about the importance of saving for periods later in life when we want to retire and enjoy life after our working years. It's why we talk about the role of insurance, investments, and emergency funds.

These are the things we talk about all the time. They are why we wrote this book.

Choices Today, Impact Tomorrow

For now, let's narrow our discussion to planning and preparation for financial independence. Retirement planning is a big part of this, as the choices and options you have later in life will be greatly influenced by the decisions you make along the way. For example, saving money on an after-tax basis through a Roth contribution within a 401(k) or 403(b) will provide you with a tax-free bucket to draw from in retirement. The alternative—making pre-tax contributions to your qualified retirement savings plan—means that when you get to retirement, what you've saved will all be taxable.

Comprehensive planning involves taking taxation into account as well as starting to save as early as possible. Because of that, when we create plans for clients during their working years, we try to maximize tax-advantaged savings so as to end up with more money in retirement. Our plans also encourage a balance between retirement funds and living funds. That is, developing a pool of money that is not specific to retirement but might be important for things like college tuition or buying a home.

It's important to also note that planning for retirement and amassing money for retirement are two different things. Both important, to be sure, but different, nonetheless. As we'll be talking about retirement planning issues throughout the book, let's first spend some time looking at how we amass money for retirement.

A person's approach to saving and investing often changes greatly over time. In our thirties, we can typically afford to invest more aggressively as we still have our entire earnings career ahead of us and plenty of time. With time on our side, our day-to-day life isn't necessarily affected by large, sudden market corrections such as those seen in 2008 and 2020.

But as we are nearing retirement, the view is completely different. A major market downturn now represents more than "paper losses." We count on those balances in our retirement accounts to supply the money to cover our day-to-day lifestyle. Suddenly, a market correction of 20 to 30 percent makes it harder to "stay the course" than it did when we were younger and had time to recover from a market decline. Retirees don't have that luxury. The money they have now has to last as long as they do. The traditional safety net available in our younger years—working more years, working longer hours, taking on a second job—has disappeared.

This is why people nearing or in retirement have to be mindful of the stability of their investments in order to provide steady cash flow and growth. The emphasis now is on protecting what you've saved while still investing for at least some growth.

It's also our belief that retirees who know they have reliable, sustainable income—money that will last as long as they do—can enjoy their retirement knowing the short-term swings of the market won't affect their income and thus their ability to live the life they achieved.

Our planning process also includes contingency planning, something we wish we could have done for the fictional Jared and people like him.

Contingency planning is important so that an unforeseen event doesn't disrupt one's entire financial plan. For example, let's say you are saving for you and your spouse's retirement when you learn that your spouse is diagnosed with ALS and will not be able to live easily in the house you currently have. Now you have to install ramps and do other renovations on the house to adapt it for a disabled person, and you will likely need at least some in-home nursing care. If your financial plan didn't include emergency reserves or a rainy-day fund, this might have a huge impact on your own ability to retire someday.

A good financial advisor will help you develop such a plan and then provide a roadmap to help you see it through. They will also build in some guardrails to deal with the bumps in the road that inevitably lie ahead.

At Sapers & Wallack, we offer a full-service financial organization with experience in many insurance products ranging from annuities to life, disability, and liability insurance; investment products, both standard and alternative; taxes and estate planning. We feel we can create customized plans that truly meet our clients' needs. We are independent, which means we are unbiased about the multitude of different financial products we can offer. We have been in business for ninety years and have lived to see the plans we create come to fruition. We have learned what can go awry and how to handle those events with our clients.

We prefer to engage the family in the planning process so that everyone has a chance to express their goals, fears, and concerns about what is most important to them. Sometimes these concerns are financial and revolve around the ability to make ends meet or to retire someday. Other times they involve leaving a legacy or giving "the kids" a better start than we might have had.

Plan to Succeed

Getting to retirement without a plan is quite stressful. When accumulating assets for retirement, the biggest decisions are typically how much to save and where to invest it. But when you get to retirement and you haven't created a plan, you are now faced with creating your own distribution strategy and worrying about whether you will outlive your assets.

One of the strategies we use for people nearing retirement is covering their fixed monthly expenses with dependable income streams. (And, if feasible, we work to make sure that unexpected expenses that could come from anywhere—be it a long-term illness, the sudden loss of a job, or any other economic setback—are also covered.) This particular strategy can be accomplished through a variety of avenues such as Social Security, pensions, annuities, rental income, and bonds. Potential long-term care costs can be covered with Long Term Care Insurance (LTCI).

Consequently, having this type of strategy in place can help you to spend guilt-free in the early years of retirement—the time when we are inclined to be more active than in later years—because you know that an income stream will continue for as long as you do.

Planning for personal legacy or charitable giving is often another important part of our process.

One of the biggest regrets we sometimes see is someone who has means and the intention to leave assets to charity but never gets around to doing it. One reason this typically happens is that people often put off planning or don't want to give away money today if they fear they might run out of it twenty to thirty years from now.

We believe that clients who implement a solid income strategy coupled with LTCI can spend more freely in their early retirement years and still have assets available for legacy giving. They can help a child buy their first home, pay for school loans, donate to a charity, or contribute to any other causes important to them. By having income streams that assure they will have the money they need for as long as they need it, they can experience the enjoyment and satisfaction of your gifting while they are still with us rather than leaving a larger chunk behind when they pass.

A final note on financial confidence: Investment performance helps people get closer to achieving their financial goals, but living within one's means and beginning to save at an early age can be even more powerful in achieving one's financial goals.

Potential Risks
to Your Ideal Retirement

Ever feel like life gets in the way and prevents you from doing things you should not ignore? If we're honest with ourselves, we've all put off obligations we know are important.

In your case, you may be reading this book because it's time to get serious about financial planning and, specifically, devising a way to best prepare for retirement. A retirement plan should be based on more components than just your investments or your finances. The preparation of that strategy begins with your desires, ambitions, and goals for this fulfilling season of life.

There's no such thing as a silly question. Not when one of the most common questions we hear from folks regarding retirement is, "Am I going to be okay?" Often, it seems, people are reluctant to meet with financial advisors because they worry they might sound uneducated. Yet, it's understandable for you to be a novice when it comes to financial issues and retirement concerns. You've been busy with your lives and your careers. Time spent away from work has meant time spent being around those you love and engaging in the activities you enjoy. Retirement provides the opportunity to do even more of that, while not fretting over work obligations.

Concerns people have about what they may encounter during retirement can be far-reaching and still perfectly legitimate. For a quick snapshot, we want to provide a brief sampling of wide-ranging issues that can arise while trying to achieve financial independence. This book will touch on many of these issues in further detail.

Politics: A presidential election often stirs emotions regarding potential effects on the economy. Investors grow anxious about how a new president can influence market returns. It's Congress, however, that establishes tax laws and passes spending bills. Yet the president can indirectly affect the economy and the stock market in various ways such as the appointment of policymakers, development of international relations, and influential sway on new legislation.

Taxes: An example of a president's influence can be cited in signature legislation passed during Donald Trump's presidency, the Tax Cuts and Jobs Act of 2017 that reduced marginal tax rates and increased the standard deduction used by many Americans. However, our tax system remains progressive, so the more you earn, the higher the tax rate within each tax bracket of subsequently higher income. A thorough understanding of tax regulations can be crucial. A financial advisor can help identify potential issues a tax professional can help solve.

Inflation: Government spending, which most recently spiked with relief packages designed to assist U.S. citizens during the COVID-19 pandemic, can fuel concerns of inflationary hikes due to an influx of money that makes its way into the economy. A retiree's income can be impacted by the effect inflation can have on a fixed budget.

Cybersecurity: Think you'll give up your smartphone in retirement? No way, right? It's here to stay, along with other intellectual gadgetry, including devices that have not been patented or invented. Retirees are becoming more tech-savvy, yet they can also be more trusting, which can be problematic when responding to potential scammers by phone, text, or email. Cybercrime often uses technology to target potential victims, many of whom are older and retired. Scammers, much like technology, figure to only grow more sophisticated over time.

CHAPTER 2

The Challenges of Longevity

You would think the prospect of our demise would loom most frightening as we age, yet many retirees say their number one concern is actually running out of money in their twilight years.[1] This fear is, unfortunately, justified, in part, because of one significant factor: We're living longer.

According to the Social Security Administration's 2011 Trustee Report, in 1950, the average life expectancy for a sixty-five-year-old man was seventy-eight, and the average for a sixty-five-year-old woman was eighty-one. In the 2022 Trustees Report issued by the SSA, those averages were eighty-three and eighty-five, respectively.[2]

The bottom line of many retirees' budget woes comes down to this: They just didn't plan to live so long. When we are younger and in our working years, living longer is not seen as a bad thing; don't some people fantasize about living forever or, at least, reaching the ripe old age of one hundred?

However, with a longer lifespan, we face a few snags. Our resources are finite—we only have so much money to provide income—but our lifespans can be unpredictably long, perhaps longer than our resources allow. Also, living longer doesn't necessarily equate with healthier lives. The longer you live, the more money you will likely need to spend on health care, even excluding long-term care needs like nursing homes.

You will also run into inflation. If you don't plan to live another twenty-five years but end up doing so, inflation at an average of 3 percent will approximately double the cost of living over that time period. To put a harsh twist on that, the buying power of a ninety-year-old will be half of what it was at sixty-five.[3]

The other potential risk we run into (because we don't necessarily get to have our cake and eat it too) is that our increased longevity puts us at risk for more health issues later in life. Typically, our need for additional care happens as we get older. Think of common situations like needing a pacemaker at eighty-five, or cancer treatment at seventy-eight.

"Wow, Aviva," we can hear you say. "You and Andrew sure have a way of leading with the good news first."

We know, we've painted a grim picture, yet all we're concerned about here is cost. It's hard to put a dollar sign on life, but that is essentially what we're talking about when discussing longevity and finances. Living longer isn't a bad thing; it just costs more, and one key to a sound retirement strategy is preparing for it in advance.

We have a client we consider a shining example of what it means to prepare for longevity.

This woman initially wanted to retire as young as possible, the sooner the better. This was priority number one in her life as she was unmarried with no kids. She was able to create a nest egg of about $2.5 million and needed it to last her lifetime. But the thought of retiring at age fifty-six was daunting because she knew that if the markets didn't cooperate and there were prolonged downturns, she would have an issue meeting her expenses in her later years.

One of the ways we were able to mitigate this anxiety was putting together a plan that was not entirely dependent upon the market and shifted some of the risk off her balance sheet. We were able to do this because she did not have to have high returns for her plan to succeed, but she did need to avoid a large drop in value. By shifting a portion of her assets into a fixed index annuity—an insurance-backed vehicle that guarantees income while protecting against loss of invested principal due to market volatility—and deferring the need to take income from her other investment accounts for ten years, we knew that she could live off the annuity income and Social Security while having her investment assets available for the reminder of her lifetime. The remaining portion of her assets were invested in equities that were earmarked for growth. Because this money was not needed for immediate lifestyle expenses, it had the time needed to withstand the volatility of the stock market.

Why could she get more mileage out of her retirement assets than most? Because her basic lifetime expenses were covered by money that was not directly exposed to market risk. This meant that the remaining assets she had invested were able to grow and had the time horizon to do so. By doing this, she could retire early, cover her life expenses, and take advantage of the growth of her discretionary monies. She used this additional money to help other family members who were less fortunate, as well as do some charitable gifting. She could also splurge more on herself, especially with some travel she had hoped to do for a long time.

Living longer may be more expensive, but it can be so meaningful when you plan for your "just-in-cases."

Retiring Early

A key part of planning for retirement revolves around retirement income. After all, retirement is cutting the cord that tethers you to your employer—and your monthly check.

However, that check often comes with many other benefits, particularly health care. Health care is often the thing that can unexpectedly put dreams for an early retirement on hold. Some employers offer health benefits to their retired workers, but that number has declined drastically over the past several decades. In 1988, among employers who offered health benefits to their workers, 66 percent offered health benefits to their retirees. In 2022, that number was 21 percent.[4]

So, with employer-offered retirement health benefits on the wane, this becomes a major point of concern for anyone who is looking to retire, particularly those who are looking to retire before age sixty-five, when they would become eligible for Medicare coverage. Fidelity estimates that the average retired couple at age sixty-five will need approximately $315,000 for health care expenses in retirement, not including long-term care.[5] Do you think it's likely that cost will decrease?

Even if you are working until age sixty-five or have plans to cover your health expenses until that point, we often have clients who incorrectly assume Medicare is their golden ticket to cover all expenses. That is simply not the case.

Retiring Later

Planning for a long life in retirement partly depends on when you retire. While many people end up retiring earlier than they anticipated—due to injuries, layoffs, family crises, and other unforeseen circumstances—continuing to work past age sixty-five is still a viable option for others and can be an excellent way to help establish financial confidence in later years.

There are many reasons for this. You still earn a paycheck and the benefits accompanying it. Medical coverage and beefing up your retirement accounts with additional savings can be significant by themselves but continuing your income also should keep you from dipping into your retirement funds, further allowing them the opportunity to grow.

Additionally, for many workers, their nine-to-five job is more than just clocking in and out. Having a sense of purpose can keep us active physically, mentally, and socially. That kind of activity and level of engagement may also help stave off many of the health problems that plague retirees. Avoiding a

16

sedentary life is one of the advantages of staying plugged into the workforce, if possible.

We have one client who retired at fifty-four years old because he was financially stable and wanted to travel and see the world while he was still young. But after a year, he found himself bored in retirement. None of his peers were retired, and after a few big trips, he was looking for things to do. He ended up going back to work part-time. He did so because he enjoyed it, but soon found that as a part-time worker, he no longer had nearly as many responsibilities as he once had. Those responsibilities, it turns out, were things he rather enjoyed and now missed. So, he ended up retiring once again.

Health Care

Take a second to reflect on your health care plan. Although working up to or even past age sixty-five would allow you to avoid a coverage gap between your working years and Medicare, that may not be an option for you. Even if it is, when you retire, you will need to make some decisions about what kind of insurance coverage you may need to supplement your Medicare. Are there any medical needs you have that may require coverage in addition to Medicare? Did your parents or grandparents have any inherited medical conditions you might consider using a special savings plan to cover?

These are all questions that are important to review with your financial advisor so you can be sure you have enough money put aside for health care.

Long-Term Care

Longevity means the need for long-term care is statistically more likely to happen. If you intend to pass on a legacy, planning for long-term care is paramount, since most estimates project nearly 70 percent of Americans will need some type of long-term care.[6] However, this may be one of the biggest, most stressful pieces of longevity planning we encounter in our work. For one thing, who wants to talk about what will happen if they can no longer toilet, bathe, dress, or feed themselves?

We get it; this is a less-than-fun part of planning. But a little bit of preparation now can go a long way!

When it comes to your longevity, just like with your other goals, a helpful thing to do is sit and dream. It may not be the fun, road-trip-to-the-Grand-Canyon kind of dreaming, but you can spend time envisioning how you want your twilight years to look.

For instance, if it is important for you to live in your home for as long as possible, who will provide for the day-to-day fixes and to-dos of housework if you become ill? Will you set aside money for a service, or do you have relatives or friends nearby whom you could comfortably allow to help you? Do you prefer in-home care over a nursing home or assisted living? This could be a good time to discuss the possibility of moving into a retirement community versus staying where you are, or whether it's worth moving to another state and leaving relatives behind.

These are all important factors to discuss with your spouse and children, as *now* is the right time to address questions and concerns. For instance, is aging in place more important to one spouse than the other? Are the friends or relatives who live nearby emotionally, physically, and financially capable of helping you for a time if you face an illness?

Many families we meet with find these conversations very uncomfortable, particularly when children discuss nursing home care with their parents. A knee-jerk reaction for many is to promise they will care for their aging parents. This is noble and well-intentioned, but there needs to be an element of realism here. Does "help" from an adult child mean they stop by and help you with laundry, cooking, home maintenance, and bills? Or does it mean they move you into their spare room when you have hip surgery? Are they prepared to help you use the restroom and bathe if that becomes difficult for you to do on your own?

We don't mean to discourage families from caring for their own; this can be a profoundly admirable relationship when it works out. However, we've seen families put off planning for late-in-life care based on a tenuous promise that adult children would care for their parents, only to watch as the support system crumbles. Sometimes this is because the assumed caregiver hasn't given serious thought to the preparation they would need, both in a formal sense and regarding their personal physical, emotional, and financial commitments. This is often also because we can't see the future: Alzheimer's disease and other maladies of old age can exact a heavy toll. When a loved one reaches the point where he or she is at risk of wandering away or needs help with two or more activities of daily living, it can be more than one person or family can realistically handle.

If you know what you want, communicate with your family about both the best-case and worst-case scenarios. Then, hope for the best, and plan for the worst.

Realistic Cost of Care

Wrapped up in your planning should be a consideration for the cost of long-term care. The potential costs for such care and treatment can be underestimated, especially by those who have maintained robust health and find it difficult to envision future declines to their condition.

Another piece of planning for long-term care costs is anticipating inflation. It's common knowledge that prices have been and keep rising, which will lower your purchasing power on everything from food to medical care. Long-term care has not escaped inflation either.

While local costs vary from state to state, following is the national median for various forms of long-term care (plus projections that account for a 3 percent annual inflation, so you can see what we are referencing):[7]

Long-Term Care Costs: Inflation			
	Home Health Care, Homemaker Services	Adult Day Care	Assisted Living	Nursing Home (semi-private room)
Annual 2021	$59,488	$20,280	$54,000	$94,900
Annual 2031	$79,947	$27,255	$72,571	$127,538
Annual 2041	$107,442	$36,628	$97,530	$171,400
Annual 2051	$144,393	$49,225	$131,072	$230,347

Fund Your Long-Term Care

A crucial mistake we see are those who haven't planned for long-term care because they assume the government will provide everything. But that's a big misconception. The government has two health insurance programs: Medicare and Medicaid. These can greatly assist you in your health care needs in retirement but usually don't provide enough coverage to cover all your health care costs in retirement. Our firm isn't a government outpost, so we don't get to make decisions when it comes to forming policy and specifics about either one of these programs. We're going to give an overview of both, but if you want to dive into the details of these programs, you can visit www.Medicare.gov and www.Medicaid.gov.

Medicare

Medicare covers those aged sixty-five and older and those who are disabled. Medicare's coverage of any nursing-home-related health issues is limited. It might cover your nursing home stay if it is not a "custodial" stay, and it isn't long-term. For example, if you break a bone or suffer a stroke, stay in a nursing home for rehabilitative care, and then return home, Medicare may cover you. But, if you have developed dementia or are looking to move to a nursing facility because you can no longer bathe, dress, toilet, feed yourself, or take care of your hygiene, etc., then Medicare is not going to pay for your nursing home costs.[8]

You can enroll in Medicare anytime during the three months before and three months after your sixty-fifth birthday. Miss your enrollment deadline, and you could risk paying increased premiums for the rest of your life.[9] On top of prompt enrollment, there are a few other things to think about when it comes to Medicare, not least among them being the need to understand the different "parts," what they do, and what they don't cover.

Part A

Medicare Part A is what you might think of as "classic" Medicare. Hospital care, some types of home health care, and major medical care fall under this. While most enrollees pay nothing for this service (as they likely paid into the system for at least ten years), you may end up paying, either based on work history or delayed signup. In 2023, the highest premium is $506 per month, and a hospital stay does have a deductible, $1,600.[10] And, if you have a hospital stay that surpasses sixty days, you could be looking at additional costs; keep in mind, Medicare doesn't pay for long-term care and services.

Part B

Medicare Part B is an essential piece of wrap-around coverage for Medicare Part A. It helps pay for doctor visits and outpatient services. This also comes with a price tag: Although the Part B deductible is only $226 in 2023, you will still pay 20 percent of all costs after that, with no limit on out-of-pocket expenses. The Part B monthly premium for 2023 ranges from the standard amount of $164.90 to $560.50.[11]

Part C

Medicare Part C, more commonly known as Medicare Advantage, is an alternative that features a combination of Parts A, B, and sometimes D. Administered through private insurance companies, these various plans have a variety of costs and restrictions, and they are subject to the specific policies and rules of the issuing carrier.

Part D

Medicare Part D is also offered through a private insurer and is supplemental to Parts A and B, as its primary purpose is to cover prescription drugs. Like any private insurance plan, Part D has its quirks and rules that vary from insurer to insurer.

The Donut Hole

Even with a "Part D" in place, you may still have a coverage gap between what your Part D private drug insurance pays for your prescriptions and what basic Medicare pays. In 2023, the coverage gap is $4,660, meaning that after you meet your private prescription insurance limit, you will spend no more than 25 percent of your drug costs out-of-pocket before Medicare will kick in to pay for more prescription drugs.[12]

Medicare Supplements

Medicare Supplement Insurance, MedSupp, Medigap, or plans labeled Medicare Part F, G, H, I, J . . . Known by a variety of monikers, this is just a fancy way of saying "medical coverage for those over sixty-five that picks up the tab for whatever the federal Medicare program(s) doesn't." Again, costs, limitations, etc., vary with each insurance carrier that offers these plans.

Does that sound like a bunch of government alphabet soup to you? It certainly does to us. And, did you read the fine print? Unpredictable costs, varied restrictions, difficult-to-compare benefits, donut holes, and coverage gaps. That's par for the course with health care plans through the course of our adult lives. What gives? We thought Medicare was supposed to be easier, comprehensive, and at no cost!

The truth is there is probably no stage of life when health care is easy to understand.

Health care costs are one of the largest costs we have in retirement but at times it feels like you need to be a brain surgeon to understand which plan is the best one for your specific situation. Regardless of the health plan chosen, there are still plenty of out-of-pocket costs, and if there is a long-term illness, health insurance only covers the medical costs, not the caregiver expenses.

From Aviva Sapers: When my grandmother had a stroke at age eighty-two, she lost her physical abilities and had to be tube fed. My grandfather provided as much caregiver support as he could, but he could not do all that was necessary. During the more than four years of living this way, both he and my father paid out of pocket over $1 million to provide caregiver support at home. For some people, that could completely drain their retirement funds and leave the surviving spouse without enough to live on. None of this was *covered by Medicare, which covers medical costs but not those for caregivers or aids.*

The best thing you can do for yourself is to scope out the health care field early, compare costs often, and prepare for out-of-pocket costs well in advance—decades, if possible.

Medicaid

Medicaid is a program the states administer, so funding, protocol, and limitations vary. Compared to Medicare, Medicaid more widely covers nursing home care, but it targets a different demographic: those with low incomes.

If you have more assets than the Medicaid limit in your state and need nursing home care, you will need to use those assets to pay for your care. You will also have a list of additional state-approved ways to spend some of these assets over the Medicaid limit, such as pre-purchasing burial plots and funeral expenses or paying off debts. After that, your remaining assets fund your nursing home stay until they are gone, at which point Medicaid will jump in.

Some people aren't stymied by this, thinking they will just pass on their financial assets early, gifting them to relatives, friends, and causes so they can qualify for Medicaid when they need it. However, to prevent this exact scenario, Uncle Sam has implemented the "look-back period." Currently, if you enroll in Medicaid, you are subject to having the government scrutinize the last five years of your finances for large gifts or expenses that may subject you to penalties, temporarily making you ineligible for Medicaid coverage.

So, if you're planning to preserve your money for future generations and retain control of your financial resources during your lifetime, you'll probably want to prepare for the costs of longevity beyond a "government plan."

Self-Funding

One way to fund a longer life is the old-fashioned way, through self-funding. There are a variety of financial tools you can use, and they all have their pros and cons. If your assets are in low-interest financial vehicles (savings, bonds, CDs), you risk letting inflation erode the value of your dollar. Or, if you are relying on the stock market, you have more growth potential, but you'll also want to consider the possible implications of market volatility. What if your assets take a hit? If you suffer a loss in your retirement portfolio in early or mid-retirement, you might have the option to "tighten your belt," so to speak, and cut back on discretionary spending to allow your portfolio the room to bounce back. But, if you are retired and depend on income from a stock account that just hit a downward stride, what are you going to do?

HSAs

These days, you might also be able to self-fund through a health savings account, or HSA, if you have access to one through a high-deductible health plan. (Note: you will not qualify to save in an HSA after enrolling in Medicare). In an HSA, any growth of your tax-deductible contributions will be tax-free, and any distributions paid out for qualified health costs are also tax-free. Long-term care expenses count as health costs, so, if this is an option available to you, it is one way to use the tax advantages to self-fund your longevity. Bear in mind, if you are younger than sixty-five, any money you use for non-qualified expenses will be subject to taxes and penalties, and, if you are older than sixty-five, any HSA money you use for non-medical expenses is subject to income tax.

LTCI

One slightly more nuanced way to pay for the potential costs of a long-term illness is with long-term care insurance, or LTCI. Just as car insurance protects your assets in case of a car accident and home insurance protects your assets in case something happens to your house, long-term care insurance aims to protect your assets in case you need long-term care services at-home or in a nursing home situation.

As with other types of insurance, you will pay a monthly or annual premium in exchange for an insurance company paying for long-term care costs down the road. Typically, policies cover three to five years of care, which is adequate for an "average" situation: it's estimated 70 percent of Americans will need about three years of long-term care of some kind.

Now, there are a few oft-cited components of LTCI that make it unattractive for some:

- Expense — LTCI can be expensive. It is generally less expensive the younger you are, but a sixty-five-year-old couple who purchased LTCI in 2023 could expect to pay a combined amount of $9,575 each year for an average three-year coverage policy.[13] And the annual cost only increases from there the older you are.

- Limited options — Let's face it: LTCI may be expensive for consumers, but it can also be expensive for companies that offer it. With fewer companies willing to take on that expense, the number of carriers to choose from is limited.

- If you know you need it, you might not be able to get it — Insurance companies offering LTCI are taking on a risk that you may need LTCI. That risk is the foundation of the product—you may or may not need it. If you know you will need it because you have a dementia diagnosis or another illness for which you will need long-term care, you will likely not qualify for LTCI coverage.

- Use it or lose it—If you have LTCI and are in the minority of Americans who die having never needed long-term care, all the money you paid into your LTCI policy is gone.

- Possibly fluctuating rates—Your rate is not locked in on LTCI. Companies maintain the ability to raise your premium amounts. This means some seniors face an ultimatum: Keep funding a policy at what might be a less affordable rate *or* lose coverage and let go of all the money they paid so far.

After that, you might be thinking, "How can people possibly be interested in LTCI?" But to repeat a point—as many as 70 percent of Americans will need long-term care. And, although only one in ten Americans age fifty-five-plus have purchased LTCI, keep in mind the high cost of care. Can you afford $7,000 a month to put into nursing home care and still have enough left over to protect your legacy? This is a very real concern considering one set of statistics reported a two-in-three chance that a senior citizen will become physically or cognitively impaired in their lifetime.[14] So, not to sound like a broken record, but it is vitally important to have a plan in place to deal with longevity and long-term care if you intend to leave a financial legacy.

From Aviva Sapers: Having had three grandparents with long-term illnesses, two in-laws who also had long-term illnesses, and a mother who needed round-the-clock care for her last few years, I am a huge proponent of LTCI. And yes, I purchased some for myself and my family, and offer a plan for my staff through work. Not only will LTCI help minimize the depletion of other assets, it also provides a roadmap on how to get proper care when needed.

A few relevant statistics to keep in mind:
- The longer you live, the more likely you are to continue living; the longer you live, the more health care you will likely need to pay for.
- The average cost of a private nursing home room in the United States in 2021 was $9,034 a month.[15] But keep

in mind, that is just the nursing home—it doesn't include other medical costs, let alone pleasantries, like entertainment or hobby spending.

- In 2022, Fidelity calculated that a healthy couple retiring at age sixty-five could expect to pay around $315,000 over the course of retirement to cover health and medical expenses.

We know; we can almost hear you saying at this point: Whoa there, folks. I was only hoping to get a realistic idea of health costs, not be driven over by a cement mixer!

The good news is, while we don't know these exact costs in advance, we do know there *will* be costs. And, you won't have to pay your total Medicare lifetime premiums in one day as a lump sum. But now that you have a good idea of health care costs in retirement, you can *plan* for them! That's the real point, here: Planning in advance can keep you from feeling nickel-and-dimed to your wits' end. Instead, having a sizable portion of your assets earmarked for health care can allow you the freedom to choose health care networks, coverage options, and long-term care possibilities you like and that you think offer you the best in life.

Product Riders[16]

LTCI and self-funding are not the only ways to plan for the expenses of longevity. Some companies are getting creative with their products, particularly insurance companies. One way they are retooling to meet people's needs is through optional product riders on annuities and life insurance. Elsewhere in this book, we talk about annuity basics, but here's a brief overview: Annuities are insurance contracts. You pay the insurance company a premium, either as a lump sum or as a series of payments over a set amount of time, in exchange for guaranteed income payments. One of the advantages of an annuity is it has access to riders, which allow you to tweak your contract for a fee, usually about 1 percent of the contract value annually. One annuity rider some companies offer is a long-term care rider. If you have an annuity with a long-term care rider and are not in need of long-term care, your contract behaves as any annuity contract would—nothing changes. Generally speaking, if you reach a point when you can't perform multiple functions of daily life on your own, you notify the insurance company, and a representative will turn on those provisions of your contract.

Like LTCI, different companies and products offer different options. Some annuity long-term care riders offer coverage of two years in a nursing home situation. Others cap expenses at two times the original annuity's value. It greatly depends. Some people prefer this option because there isn't a "use-it-or-lose-it" piece; if you die without ever having needed long-term care, you still will have had the income benefit from the base contract. Still, as with any annuities or insurance contracts, there are the usual restrictions and limitations. Withdrawing money from the contract will affect future income payments, early distributions can result in a penalty, income taxes may apply, and, because the insurance company's solvency is what guarantees your payments, it's important to do your research about the insurance company from which you are considering purchasing a contract.

Understandably, a discussion on long-term care is bound to feel at least a little tedious. Yet, this is a critical piece of planning for income in retirement, particularly if you want to leave a legacy.

No one wants to plan for health issues in retirement...unless they have experienced it first hand by taking care of a parent. Even then, most meetings involving LTCI discussions head in one of two directions. People either say "It costs too much," or "The cost doesn't matter. I do not want to be a burden to my children."

The problem that comes with long-term care is not only a financial one, but also an emotional and lifestyle concern. You can often tell in the tone of voice of someone who is caring for an aging family member that the situation is more than they can handle. We also sense an elder parent's guilt for being a burden and the adult child's resentment. This is, after all, not what they want to be doing with their free time.

This can become an even bigger issue when someone needs round-the-clock care and they don't have the money to pay for it. Typically, this is when the children try to step in and help their parents, but doing so can put a financial strain on them as well. This creates another layer of resentment within siblings.

People who seek non-family care also face a daunting task in trying to pay for this expensive help.

One of our clients, for example, lives in a home worth roughly $1.5 million, but is widowed and ninety years old with no other money to her name. She is adamant that she does not want to sell the family home, one she has lived in for the last seventy years, and move to an assisted living/nursing facility. She would prefer that someone come to the house daily to assist her with the activities of daily living.

But where will the money come from to pay for these services? She did not purchase an LTC policy when she was younger, so she now has to pay out of pocket for any in-home care. But with little to no money in the bank, her only asset is her home and whatever money she can take from its value. This equity has a limit, however, and we project that she will run out of money if she reaches age ninety-six. At this point, her family will have to come in to support her in any way they can, which will likely cause a rift over who does or pays for what.

Spousal Planning

Here's one thing to keep in mind no matter how you plan to save: Many of us will be planning for more than ourselves. Look back at all the stats on health events and the likelihood of long life and long-term care. If they hold true for a single individual, then the likelihood of having a costly health or long-term care event is even higher for a married couple. You'll be planning for not just one life, but two. So, when it comes to long-term care insurance, annuities, self-funding, or whatever strategy you are looking at using, be sure you are funding longevity for the both of you.

CHAPTER 3

Retirement Income

R etirement. For many of us, it's what we've saved for and
dreamed of, pinning our hopes to a magical someday. Is
that someday full of traveling? Is it filled with
grandkids? Gardening? Maybe your fondest dream is simply
never having to work again, never having to clock in or be
accountable to someone else.

Your ability to do these things all hinges on *income*.
Without the money to support these dreams, even a basic level
of work-free lifestyle is unsustainable. That's why planning for
an income stream in retirement is so foundational, but where
do we begin?

It's easy to feel overwhelmed by this question. Some may
feel the urge to amass a large lump sum and then try to put it
all in one strategy —insurance, investments, liquid assets—to
provide all the growth, liquidity, and income they need.
Instead, we think you need a balanced approach. After all,
retirement planning isn't magic. As we mention elsewhere,
there is no single product that can be all things to all people
(or even all things to one person). No approach works
unilaterally for everyone.

That's why it's important to look at different strategies with
someone who is an expert in the field of retirement planning
and see what works best for you and your family. Not only will
you have the assurance that you have addressed the areas you
need to, but you will also have an ally who can help you break

down the process and help keep you from feeling overwhelmed.

Sources of Income

Thinking of all the pieces in your retirement plan might seem intimidating. But, like cleaning out a junk drawer or revisiting that garage remodel, once you have laid everything out, you can begin to sort things into categories.

Once you have a good overall picture of where your expenses will lie, you can start stacking up the resources to cover them.

Social Security

Social Security is a guaranteed, inflation-protected federal insurance program that plays a significant part in most of our retirement plans. From delaying when to start taking your first distribution to examining spousal benefits, as we discuss in a separate chapter elsewhere in this book, there is plenty you can do to try to make the most of this monthly benefit. As with all your retirement income sources, it's important to consider how to make this resource stretch to provide the most bang and buck.

Pension

Another generally reliable source of guaranteed retirement income might be a pension.

If you are one of the lucky people who still has a pension, they can be such a central piece of your retirement income plan and you will want to put some thought into answering basic questions about it.

How well is your pension funded? There are many instances in the past where companies and governments have neglected to fund their pension obligations, causing a persistent problem with this otherwise reliable form of retirement income. However, research conducted by the Pew Charitable Trusts showed a collective increase in assets exceeding half a trillion dollars in state retirement plans fueled by strong market investment returns in fiscal 2021. Pew's estimates that state retirement systems rose to 80 percent funding for the first time in 2008.[17]

Consider the factors at play, though. Pensions had been underfunded but gained a boost from strong market performance in 2021. But what happens to the solvency of those pension funds if the market declines?

It can be worthwhile to keep tabs on your pension fund's health and know what your options are for withdrawing your pension. Typically, you have one chance at electing the distribution option at your retirement with no recourse to change at a later date, so you will want to look at all options before making a final decision. If you have already retired and made those decisions, this is likely a foregone conclusion. If not, it pays to know what you can expect and what decisions you can make, such as taking spousal options to cover your husband or wife if he or she outlives you.

Your 401(k) and IRA

One "modern way" to save for retirement is in a 401(k) or IRA, or their nonprofit or governmental equivalents, the 403(b) and TSP (Thrift Savings Plan. It can be a mistake not to take full advantage of opportunities to invest in an employer-sponsored 401(k) or your own Individual Retirement Account. Yet according to one article, only 32 percent of Americans invest in a 401(k), though 59 percent of employed Americans have access to this option.[18]

Also, if you have changed jobs over the years, do the work of tracking down any benefits from your past employers. You might have an IRA here or a 401(k) there; keep track of those so you can pull them together and look at those assets when you're ready to look at establishing sources of retirement income.

Do You Have...

- Life insurance?
- Annuities?
- Long-term care insurance?
- Any passive income sources?
- Stock and bond portfolios?
- Liquid assets? (What's in your bank account?)
- Alternative investments?
- Rental properties?

It's important to look at your full retirement income picture and pull together *all* your assets, no matter how big or small. From the free insurance policy offered through your work to the sizable investment in your brother-in-law's modestly successful furniture store, you want to have a good idea of where your money is.

This process of assembling all of your income sources and then seeing the total in black and white not only helps clarify your financial picture but can often pleasantly surprise you. Many people we've worked with, after going through the income discovery part of our financial planning process, have looked at the bottom line and been stunned by what they see. "Wow, look at that. I'm a millionaire!" we've heard on many different occasions. It's a fun part of what we do.

More people than you would think greatly underestimate their net worth. This happens for a variety of reasons, one being that they have never seen the number until we show them. Another is that people discount the value of their homes. Here in the greater Boston area, home values can be a large part of someone's net worth. Your home is typically one of, if not the highest, source of net worth. This is an asset that should not be overlooked, even if it is not yet cash in hand.

Retirement Income Needs

How much income will you need in retirement? How do you determine that? A lot of people work toward a random number, thinking, "If I just had a million dollars, I'd be comfortable in retirement!" Don't get us wrong; it is possible to save up a lot of money and then retire in the hopes you can keep your monthly expenses lower than some set estimation. But this carries a general risk of running out of money. Instead, we work with our clients to find out what their current and projected income needs are and then work from there to see how we might cover any gaps between what they have and what they want.

Goals and Dreams

We like to start with your pie in the sky aspirations. Do you find yourself planning for your vacations more thoroughly than you do your retirement? It's not uncommon for Americans to do exactly that. Maybe it's because planning a vacation is less stressful: Having a week at the beach going awry is, well, a walk on the beach compared to running out of money in retirement. Whatever the case, perhaps it would be better if you thought of your retirement as a vacation in and of itself—no clocking in, no boss, no overtime. If you felt unlimited by financial strain, what would you do?

Would an endless vacation for you mean Paris and Rome? Would it mean mentoring at children's clubs or serving at the local soup kitchen? Or maybe it would mean deepening your ties to those immediately around you—neighbors, friends, and family. Maybe it would mean more time to take part in the hobbies and activities you love. Have you been considering a second (or even third) act as a small-business owner, turning a hobby or passion into a revenue source?

This is your time to daydream and answer the question: If you could do anything, what would you do?

After that, it's a matter of putting a dollar amount on it. What are the costs of round-the-world travel? One couple we know said their highest priority in retirement was being able to take each of their grandchildren on a cross-country vacation every year. That's a pretty specific goal—one that is reasonably easy to nail down a budget for.

From Andrew MacDougall: Our clients have specific goals involving charitable giving. One couple that comes to mind wanted to see and enjoy the results of their giving while they were still here to do so and asked us to help make that possible. We restructured some of their assets to provide income streams that would last throughout their lifetimes, leaving them in position to make charitable contributions today without having to think, "Maybe I shouldn't have done that in 2023 if I might run out of money when I'm ninety."

We work with people to take the anxiety out of charitable giving, especially when it allows them to see the fruits of their giving today as opposed to passing on assets after they pass—something too many people, unfortunately, have to do.

Current Budget

Compiling a current expense report is one of the trickiest pieces of retirement preparation. Many people assume the expenses of their lives in retirement will be different—more specifically, lower. After all, there will be no drive to work, no need for a business wardrobe, and perhaps most impactful of all, no more saving for retirement!

Yet, we often underestimate our daily spending habits. Most people, during their working years, spend the most money on Saturdays than on other days of the week. In retirement, however, every day is a Saturday.

We can't count the number of times we have sat with a couple, asked them about their spending, and heard them throw out a number that seemed incredibly low. When we ask them where the number came from, they usually say they estimated based on their total bills. Yet, our spending is so much more than our mortgage, utilities, cable, phone, car, grocery, or credit card bills.

"What about clothes?" we ask, "Or dining out? What about gifts and coffees and last-minute birthday cards?" That's when the lights come on.

This is why we suggest collecting a year's worth of information. There is usually no such thing as a one-time purchase. Did you buy new furniture? Even if that is a rarity, do you think that will be the last time you *ever* buy furniture?

From Andrew MacDougall: We sat with a client recently who thought they only spent about $5,000 a month. But when we gathered their bank statements and investment statements, we found that they actually were spending closer to $10,000 each month. This was a huge eye-opening moment that led to a challenging discussion about living within a budget.

Another hefty expense is spending on the kids. Many of the couples we work with are quick to help their adult children, whether it's paying for college, babysitting, paying an occasional bill, contributing to a grandchild's college fund, or just letting them live in the basement. Research concluded that 22 percent of adults receive some kind of financial support from parents. That segment jumps to almost 30 percent when factoring the generation we call millennials.[19]

Our clients sometimes protest that what they do for their grown children can stop in retirement. They don't *need* our help anymore, they will say. Even so, parents like to feel needed. And while you never want to neglect saving for retirement in favor of taking on additional financial obligations (like your child's student debt), parents who help their adult children do so in part because it helps them feel fulfilled.

When it comes down to estimating expenses, including (and especially) spending on your family, don't make your initial calculations based on what you *could* whittle your budget down to if you *had* to. Instead, start from where you are. Who wants to live off a bare-bones bank account in retirement?

Other Expenses

Once you have nailed down your current budget and your dreams or goals for retirement, there are a few other outstanding pieces to think about—some expenses many people don't take the time to consider before making and executing a plan. But we're assuming you want to get it right, so let's take a look.

Housing

Do you know where you want to live in retirement? This makes up a substantial piece of your income puzzle—since the typical American household owns a home, and it's generally their largest asset.

Some people prefer to live right where they are for as long as they can. Others have been waiting for retirement to pull the trigger on an ambitious move, like purchasing a new house in a warmer climate, or even downsizing. Whatever your plans and whatever your reasons, there are quite a few things to consider.

Mortgage

Do you still have a mortgage? What may have been a nice tax boon in your working years could turn into a financial burden in your retirement. After all, when you are on a limited income, a mortgage is just one more bill weakening your financial strength. It is something to put some thought into, whether you plan to age in place or are considering moving to your dream home, buying a house out of state, or living in a retirement community.

Upkeep and Taxes

A house without a mortgage still requires annual taxes. While it's tempting to think of this as a once-a-year expense, when you have limited earning potential, your annual tax bill might be something into which you should put a little more forethought.

The costs of homeownership aren't just monetary. When you find yourself dealing with more house than you need, it can drain your time and energy. From keeping clutter at bay to keeping the lawn mower running, upkeep can be extensive and expensive. For some, that's a challenge they heartily accept and can comfortably take on. For others, the idea of yard work or cleaning an area larger than they need feels foolish.

For instance, Peggy discovered after her knee replacement that most of her house was inaccessible to her when she was laid up.

"It felt ridiculous," she said, "to pay someone else to dust and vacuum a house I was only living in 40 percent of!"

Practicality and Adaptability

Erik and Magda are looking to retire within the next two decades. They just sold their old three-bedroom ranch-style house. Their twins are in high school, and the couple has wanted to "upgrade" for years. Now they live in a gorgeous

1940s three-story house with all the kitchen space they ever wanted, five sprawling bedrooms, and a library and media room for themselves and their children. But within months of moving in, the couple realized a house perfect for their active teens would no longer be perfect for them in five to fifteen years.

"We are paying the mortgage for this house, but we've started saving for the next one," said Magda. "Seriously, who wants to climb two flights of stairs to their bedroom when they're seventy-eight?"

Others we know have encountered a similar situation in their personal lives. After a health crisis, one couple found the luxurious tub for two had become a specter of a bad slip and a potential safety risk. It's important to think through what your physical reality could be. We always emphasize to our clients that they should plan for whatever their long-term future might hold, but it's amazing how many people don't give it much thought.

Contracts and Regulations

If you are looking into a cross-country move, be aware of new tax tables or local ordinances in the area where you are looking to move. After all, you don't want to experience sticker-shock when you are looking at downsizing or reducing your bills in retirement.

Along the same lines, if you are moving into a retirement community, be sure to look at the fine print. What happens if you must move into a different arrangement or housing for long-term care? Will you be penalized? Will you be responsible for replacing your slot in the community? What are all the fees, and what do they cover?

Inflation

As we write this in 2023, America has experienced a wave of inflation following a lengthy period of low inflation. Inflation zoomed to 9.1 percent in June 2022, its highest mark since November 1981.[20]

Core inflation is yet another measurement that excludes goods with prices that tend to be more volatile, such as food and energy costs. Core inflation for a 12-month period ending in December 2022 was 5.7 percent. It so happened energy prices rose 7.3 percent over that timeframe.[21]

However, inflation isn't a one-time bump; it has a cumulative effect. Again, that can impact the price of groceries greater than other goods. Even with relatively low inflation over the past few decades, an item you bought in 1997 for two dollars will cost about $3.70 today.[22] Want to go to a show? A $20 ticket in 1997 would cost $41.24 in 2023.[23]

What if, in retirement, we hit a stretch like the late seventies and early eighties, when annual inflation rates of 10 percent became the norm? It may be wise to consider some extra padding in your retirement income plan to account for any potential increase in inflation in the future.

Aging

Also in the expense category, think about longevity. We all hope to age gracefully. However, it's important to face the prospect of aging with a sense of realism.

The elephant in the room for many families is long-term care. No one wants to admit they will likely need it, but estimates indicate almost 70 percent of us will.[24] Aging is a significant piece of retirement income planning because you'll want to figure out how to set aside money for your care, either at home or away from it. The more comfortable you get with discussing your wishes and plans with your loved ones, the easier planning for the financial side of it can be.

We discuss health care and potential long-term care costs in more detail elsewhere in this book but suffice it to say nursing home care tends to be very expensive and typically isn't something you get to choose when you need it.

It isn't just the costs of long-term care that pose a concern in living longer. It's also about covering the possible costs of everything else associated with living longer. For instance, if Henry retires from his job as a biochemical engineer at age sixty-five, perhaps he planned to have a very decent income for twenty years, until age eighty-five. But what if he lives until he's ninety-five? That's a whole third—ten years—more of personal income he will need.

Putting It All Together

Just as establishing a solid foundation is a core component of any home-building project, it is equally important when developing an income plan. To lay such a foundation, we work to help our clients figure out how to cover their day-to-day living expenses—their essential needs—with insurance and other guaranteed income sources like annuities and Social Security.

But in order to build such a foundation, we first need rock-solid information.

This means it is important that you provide accurate data. If you are spending $12,000 each month but tell us your monthly spending is only $8,000, well, that is a major problem. Many people simply fail to factor in the wide variety of miscellaneous expenses—both regular and irregular—that go into daily living. What about a new car purchase or potentially expensive repairs to your current car? What about major home renovations or simple home repairs? Additional travel? Medical expenses? And how much might you spend on the "fun things" that make life worth living—dining out, movies, club dues, the countless ways you spoil your grandkids?

Once we have an accurate estimate of your expenses, then we can set up both an income plan that meets your projected lifestyle expenses, and an investment strategy that takes assets not needed for immediate wants and needs and gives them the opportunity to grow for future ones. When this is completed, we project what each year of retirement looks like and where you are going to get the money needed to support the lifestyle you hope to live. Once we have a road map of what your retirement could look like, we can monitor whether you are on the right path or if we have to make any adjustments.

Again, you should keep in mind there isn't one single financial vehicle, asset, or source to fill all your needs, and that's okay. One of the challenges of planning for your income in retirement concerns figuring out what products and strategies to use. You can release some of that stress when you accept the fact you will probably need a diverse portfolio— potentially with bonds, stocks, insurance, and other income sources—not just one massive money pile.

It's also important to keep in mind that spending down your investment accounts is a lot different than when you were sitting and letting them grow. The financial concept of "sequence risk" comes into play here. Sequence risk suggests that the long-term performance of an investment portfolio is more adversely affected when withdrawals—such as those taken to produce income in retirement—are made when a market downturn reduces the value of the portfolio's holdings.

Think about that for a minute. When you were consistently putting money into an investment account, a market downturn allowed you to buy new shares at a lower price. Example: a $5,000 purchase of XYZ stock at $25 a share put 200 new shares into your investment portfolio. But when the price of XYZ stock drops $5 per share, that same $5,000 purchase at $20 per share now buys you 250 new shares. In short, more bang for the buck.

In retirement, however, you are more likely to be selling shares to generate income without having any "new money" flowing in. Consequently, a market downturn that reduces share value in your portfolio produces a kind of double-whammy on the money you are likely to need for either future income or legacy giving. Because you must sell more shares at a lower price to produce the income you need, your portfolio now has fewer shares that might gain in value when the market rebounds.

The point here is that a retiree must be conscious of the timing of distributions taken from an investment portfolio. Here is where we can help reduce the risk of an ill-timed decision.

Filling the 'Income Gap'

Once you have analyzed your income needs and wants, and the assets to realistically cover them, you may have an "income gap". The masterstroke of a competent financial advisor will be to help you figure out how you will cover that gap. Will you need to cut out a round of golf a week? Maybe skip the new car? Or will you need to take more substantial action?

One way to cover an income gap is to consider working longer or even part-time before retirement and even after that magical calendar date. This may not be the best "plan" for you; disabilities, work demands, and physical or emotional limitations can hinder the best-laid plans to continue working. However, if it is physically possible for you, this is one considerable way to help your assets last, for more than one reason.

In fact, 46 percent of the Americans responding to a survey report they plan to work part-time after retiring, while 18 percent indicated they planned to work past the age of seventy.[25]

But while working in retirement is always an income-producing possibility—especially if you are working because you **want to** as opposed to **having to**—the bigger joy is knowing you can experience retirement without the drudgery of the daily workplace.

Another element of filling the income gap involves knowing you have the means to cover a future expense—one we hope you never have to deal with—that has the potential to ravage your retirement savings and your retirement plan. We're talking here about the potential need for long-term care.

From Andrew MacDougall: One of our long-time clients was entering his sixties when he asked us whether he could afford to retire. We ran the numbers with assumptions that we both agreed were reasonable and gave our opinion that we didn't feel he could retire at age sixty. However, after a strong market over the next two years, we ran the numbers again and felt comfortable that he and his wife could retire at age sixty-two and would not outlive their assets. They were thrilled and immediately began talking about traveling more and spending more time with their grandkids.

They were able to consider all this, we believed, in part because they both had long-term care insurance. If either of them needed nursing care, they had the means to receive the care they would need without a huge negative effect on their retirement plan.

Another way to help shore up your income gap is to mitigate your tax exposure. For people with a 401(k) or IRA, a tax advisor in your corner can help you figure out how and when to take distributions from your account in a way that doesn't push you into a higher tax bracket. Or you might learn how to use tax-advantaged bonds more effectively. Effective tax planning isn't necessarily about "adding" to your income.

47

Especially regarding retirement, it's less about what you make than it is about what you keep. Paying a lower tax bill keeps more money in your pocket, which is where you want it when it comes to retirement income.

Now you can look at ways to cover your remaining retirement goals. Are there products like long-term care insurance specific to a certain kind of expense you anticipate? Is there a particular asset you want to use for your "play" money—money for trips and gifts for the grandkids? Is there any way you can portion off money for those charitable legacy plans?

When you're retired, you no longer have an employer paying you a steady check. It is up to you to make sure you have saved and planned for the income you need.

CHAPTER 4

Market Volatility

U p and down. Roller coaster. Merry-go-round. Bulls and bears. Peak-to-trough.

Sound familiar? This is the language we use to talk about the stock market. With volatility and spikes, even our language is jarring, bracing, and vivid.

Still, financial strategies tend to revolve around market-based products, for good reasons. For one thing, there is no other financial class that packs the same potential for growth, pound for pound, as stock-based products, real estate, venture capital, and private equity. Because of growth potential, inflation protection, and new opportunities, it may be unwise to avoid the market entirely.

However, along with the potential for growth is the potential for loss. At the time this book was written, many of the people we've seen in our office came in feeling uneasy because of the economic fallout of the COVID-19 outbreak of 2020, followed by the economic downturn, and the inflation spike that happened in 2022 and on into early 2023.

So, how do we balance these factors? How do we try to satisfy both the need for protection and the need for growth?

For one thing, it is important to recognize the value of diversification.[26] Now, we're not just talking about the diversity of assets among different kinds of stocks, or even different kinds of stocks and bonds. That's only one kind of diversity; while important, both stocks and bonds, though

49

different, are both still market-based products. Most market-based products, even within a diverse portfolio, tend to rise or lower as a whole, just like an incoming tide. Therefore, a portfolio diverse in only market-sourced products won't automatically protect your assets during times when the market declines.

In addition to the sort of "horizontal diversity" you have by purchasing a variety of stocks and bonds from different companies, we also suggest you think about "vertical diversity," or diversity among asset classes. This means having different product types, including securities products, bank products, real estate, and insurance products—with varying levels of growth potential, liquidity, and protection—all in accordance with your unique situation, goals, and needs.

The level of risk you are comfortable taking with your investments is another important factor in determining the diversity of an investment portfolio. Determining your specific risk tolerance—something that is unique to each client—is one of the first things we establish in designing the mix of ingredients that will go into your investment pie.[27]

Our process in determining risk tolerance involves more than simply filling out a questionnaire. We ask many additional questions so that we can determine a client's needs and timing of access to their funds. Among the many issues we will consider to determine risk tolerance:

- Upcoming large expenses (home renovation, car replacement, etc).
- Time horizon of when you would need this money; how long can you stay invested?
- What happens if there is a down market and this account is greatly diminished or depleted? In other words, are you gambling with money you can't afford to lose?
- Are you actively spending down the money in this account or letting it grow?

- Are there other people you are financially responsible for?
- Do you stay the course when the market drops? (Be honest now. Some people say they can hold the line during tough times, but when the market drops, they freak out.)
- Are you OK spending down assets if need be?
- Are you still working? Do you have access to other income if the market value of your portfolio drops?
- What happens if life gets in the way and you need this money sooner than you planned?

We approach building portfolios with a goal of minimizing market volatility as much as possible if money is earmarked to be needed within three years. We would invest such money in something relatively safe so that even if the market does crash, our clients' expenses are covered. Longer term assets can withstand more market volatility.

The Color of Money

When you're looking at the overall diversity of your portfolio, part of the equation is knowing which products fit in what category: what has liquidity, what has protection, and what has growth potential.

Before we dive in, keep in mind these aren't absolutes. You might think of liquidity, growth, and protection as primary colors. While some products will look pretty much yellow, red, or blue, others will have a mix of characteristics, making them more green, orange, or purple.

Growth

We like to think of the growth category as red. It's powerful, it's somewhat volatile, and it's also the category where the greatest opportunities exist for growth and loss. Often, products in the growth category will have a good deal of liquidity but very little protection. These are our market-based products and strategies, and we think of them mostly in shades of red and orange, to designate their growth and liquidity. This is a good place to be when you're young—think fast cars and flashy leather jackets—but its allure often wanes as you move closer to retirement. Examples of "red" products include:

- Stocks
- Equities
- Exchange-traded funds
- Mutual funds[28]
- Corporate bonds
- Real estate investment trusts[29]
- Speculations
- Alternative investments[30]

Liquidity

Yellow is our liquid category color. We typically recommend having at least enough yellow money to cover six months to a year's worth of expenses in case of emergency. Yellow assets don't need a lot of growth potential; they just need to be readily available when we need them. The "yellow" category includes assets like:

- Cash
- Money market accounts

Protection

The color of protection,[31] to us, is blue. Tranquil, peaceful, sure, even if it lacks a certain amount of flash. This is the direction we like to see people generally move toward as they're nearing retirement. The red, flashy look of stock market returns and the risk of possible overnight losses is less attractive as we near retirement and look for more consistency and reliability. While this category doesn't come with a lot of liquidity, the products here are backed by an insurance company, a bank, or a government entity. "Blue" products include things such as:

- Certificates of deposit (backed by banks)
- Government-based bonds (backed by the U.S. government)
- Life insurance (backed by insurance companies)
- Annuities (also backed by insurance companies)

The investment portfolios we build for our clients can incorporate all three "colors of money." Built upon a disciplined investment philosophy, they follow a set of guiding principles that enable a long-term view with short-term flexibility, centered on managing downside risk. They seek to deliver enhanced returns while maintaining a similar risk profile as the benchmarks to which their performance is often compared. Understanding our client's real risk tolerance allows our team of experienced investment professionals to make more informed decisions in order to better match our plans and product choices for our clients. Our team's dynamic approach to strategic asset allocation allows for the flexibility to adapt as market conditions change.[32] Active decisions are made throughout the year to ensure the right exposures and risk measures are being taken at the right time.

Let's take a moment to discuss diversification as part of an investment strategy and why strategic asset allocation is important. Diversification involves considering the many different types of investments that are available including stocks versus bonds, U.S. vs. foreign; large cap vs. small cap stocks; value vs. growth-oriented stocks; income and dividend-producing stocks vs. those with the potential for appreciation. There are also other categories like real estate, private equity, and venture capital. Your tax situation also plays a role in asset allocation decisions.

(This is material that could comprise its own book—and perhaps we'll write it someday soon—but for now just know that these are all factors that go into our investment philosophy around diversification.)

Please know too that we are not market timers. We also believe there is great value in passive investing, but in some areas, there is value added in active management. One area where we feel a manager can add value is typically in portfolios where there is a solid need for income. We're not saying our philosophy is unique, but we are big believers in diversification and in a "bucket approach" where each bucket is managed according to the time frame within which the monies will be needed.

We believe that with our background in market-based products (stocks, bonds, ETFs, etc.) as well as with all insurance-based investment products (annuities, life insurance) and private placement,[33] we are well positioned to truly customize plans for our clients. It is our belief that many investment houses that are unfamiliar with insurance-based products miss the opportunity for tax-advantaged investing. In addition, our expertise in charitable strategies also allows us to get a bit more creative for our clients.

Retirement account rules, regs, fees

We want to take a second to specifically address a method many retirees will use to build their retirement income: contributing to retirement accounts, many of them employment-related. Any of these retirement accounts (IRAs, 401(k)s, 403(b)s, TSPs, etc.) are basically "tax wrappers." What do we mean by that? Well, depending on your plan, a 401(k) could include target-date funds, passively managed products, stocks, bonds, mutual funds, or even variable, fixed, and fixed index annuities, all collected in one place and governed by rules (a.k.a. the "tax wrapper"). These rules govern how much money you can put inside, what ways you can put it in, when you will pay taxes on it, and when you can take the money out. Inside the 401(k), each of the products might have its own fees or commissions, in addition to the management fee you pay on the 401(k) itself.

Fees can be troublesome. You can't get something for nothing. Fees are how many financial companies and professionals make a living. But it's important to recognize that even a fee with only a fraction of a percentage point is money out of your pocket—money that represents not just the one-time fee of today but also an opportunity cost. A $100,000 IRA that earns 6 percent over a twenty-five-year period without investment fees would earn $430,000. But if just a 0.5 percent fee is factored into that investment, the IRA would be worth $379,000 in twenty-five years, a $50,500 decrease.[34] For someone close to retirement, how much do you think fees may have cost over their lifetime?

It's important to look at management fees and assess if you think you're getting what you pay for. Over the course of ten years, those costs can add up, and you may have decades ahead of you in which you will need to rely on your assets.

Dollar-Cost Averaging

With 401(k)s and other market-based retirement products, dollar-cost averaging is a concept that can work in your favor when you are investing for the long term. [35]When the market is trending up, if you are consistently contributing money, month over month, great; your investments can grow, and you are adding to your assets. When the market takes a dip, no problem; your dollars buy more shares at a lower price. At some point, we hope the market will rebound, in which case your shares can grow and be more valuable than they were before. This concept is what we call "dollar-cost averaging." While it can't ensure a profit or guarantee against losses, it's a time-tested strategy for investing in a volatile market.

However, when you are in retirement, this strategy may work against you. You may have heard of "reverse" dollar-cost averaging. Before, when the market lost ground, you were "bargain-shopping;" your dollars purchased more assets at a reduced price. When you are in retirement, you are no longer the purchaser; you are selling. So, in a down market, you have to sell more assets to make the same amount of money as what you made in a favorable market.

We've had lots of people step into our office to talk to us about this, emphasizing, "my advisor says the market always bounces back, and I have to just hold on for the long term."

There's some basis for this thinking; thus far, the market has always rebounded to higher heights than before. But this is no guarantee, and the prospect of potentially higher returns in five years may not be very helpful in retirement if you are relying on the income from those returns to pay this month's electric bill, for example.

At our company, we work to preserve client portfolios from market volatility by employing (among other things) dollar cost averaging, diversification strategies, and investing for the long-term with equities using the "bucket strategy" described above. But even when doing this, market volatility will always happen. If you are not prepared for it, you should not be investing your money.

Sometimes, even people who say they understand how a market will have ups and downs get more than a little nervous when the downs drop too low. We've known people who say they have an aggressive risk tolerance but suddenly become something closer to a balanced investor when their portfolio shows a large decrease. We believe determining when you will need your money should be a bigger factor than day-to-day performance when considering how that money should be invested.

We do not like to change long-term investment strategy based on short-term market volatility. We say this because even a bull market can experience short-term downturns. A good example of intra-year stock market declines is demonstrated in an analysis of annual returns cited by J.P. Morgan Asset Management. It showed several years of strong net positive annual returns that also included significant declines within the calendar year. In 1998, for example, the S&P 500 index[36] had a net annual gain of 27 percent after being down 19 percent at one time that year. In 2018, the index finished the year up 29 percent despite being down 34 percent at its low point. In 2021, the S&P 500 had a yearly return of 16 percent, but experienced an intra-year pandemic-related decline of 34 percent.[37]

Is There a "Perfect" Product?

To bring us back around to the discussion of protection, growth, and liquidity, the ideal product would be a "ten" in all three categories, right? Completely guaranteed, doubling in size every few years, and accessible whenever you want. Does such a product exist? Absolutely not.

Instead of running in circles looking for that perfect product, the silver bullet, the unicorn of financial strategies, it's more important to circle back to the concept of a balanced, asset-diverse portfolio.

This is why your interests may be best served when you work with a trusted professional who is familiar with a multitude of financial products and can help you incorporate them in your personal retirement strategy.

CHAPTER 5

Annuities

Working to achieve financial goals takes planning, and there are several financial products and strategies we typically employ to put together a complete retirement plan. In certain circumstances, we believe annuities play a role, and we use them even though we understand that many people find them mysterious. So, in the interest of demystifying annuities, let's talk a little about what they are.

An annuity is an insurance product, and like all insurance, they are designed as a financial hedge against risk. Car owners buy auto insurance to protect their finances in case they injure someone or someone injures them. Homeowners have homeowners' insurance to protect their finances in case of a fire, flood, or another disaster. People have life insurance to protect their finances in case of untimely death. Almost juxtaposed to life insurance, people have annuities in case of a long life, as annuities can give you financial protection by providing consistent and reliable income payments.

The basic premise of an annuity is that you, the annuitant, pay an insurance company some amount in exchange for their contractual guarantee to pay you income for a certain time period. How that company pays you, for how long, and how much they offer are all determined by the annuity contract you enter into with the insurance company.

How You Get Paid

There are two ways for an annuity contract to provide income: The first is through what is called annuitization, and the second is through the use of income riders. We'll get into income riders in a bit, but let's talk about annuitization. That nice, long word is, in our opinion, one reason annuities have a reputation for mystery and misinformation.

Annuitization

When someone "annuitizes" a contract, it is the point where he or she turns on the income stream. Once a contract has been annuitized, there is no going back. With annuities, if the policyholder lives longer than the insurance company planned, the insurance company is still obligated to pay him or her, even if the payments end up being way more than the contract's actual value. If, however, the policyholder dies an untimely death, depending on the contract type, the insurance company may keep anything left of the money that funded the annuity—nothing would be paid out to the contract holder's survivors. You see where that could make some people balk?

Now, modern annuities rarely rely on annuitization for the income portion of the contract. They instead have so many bells and whistles that the old concept of annuitization seems outdated, but because this is still an option, it's important to at least understand the basic concept.

Riders

Speaking of bells and whistles, let's talk about annuity riders. Modern annuities have a lot of different options these days, many in the form of riders you can add to your contract for a fee—usually about 1 percent of the contract value per year. Each rider has its particulars, and the types of riders available will vary by the type of annuity contract purchased, but let's just briefly outline some of these little extras:

- Lifetime income rider: Contract guarantees you an income for life.
- Death benefit rider: Contract pays an enhanced death benefit to your beneficiaries even if you have annuitized it.
- Return of premium rider: Guarantees you (or your beneficiaries) will at least receive back the amount paid for the annuity.
- Long-term care rider: Provides a certain amount, sometimes as much as twice the normal income benefit amount, for a period of time to help pay for long-term care if the contract holder is moved to a nursing home or assisted living situation.

This isn't an extensive look, and usually the riders have fancier names based on the issuing company, like "ABC Insurance Company Income Preferred Bonus Fixed Index Annuity rider." But we just wanted to show you what some of the general options are in layperson's terms.

Types of Annuities

Annuities break down into four basic types: immediate, variable, fixed, and fixed index.

Immediate

Immediate annuities primarily rely on annuitization to provide income—you give the insurance company a lump sum up front, and your payments begin immediately. Once you begin receiving income payments, the transaction is irreversible, and you no longer have access to your money in a lump sum. When you die, any remaining contract value is typically forfeited to the insurance company.

All other annuity contract types are "deferred" contracts, meaning you fund your policy as a lump sum over a period of years, and it grows over years or decades.

Variable

A variable annuity is an insurance contract as well as an investment.[38] It's sold by insurance companies, but only through someone who is registered to sell investment products. With a variable annuity contract, the insurance company invests your premiums in subaccounts that are tied to the stock market. This makes it a bit different from the other annuity contract types because it is the only contract where your money is subject to losses because of market declines. Your contract value has a greater opportunity to grow, but it also stands to lose. Additionally, your contract's value will be subject to the underlying investment fees and management fees, etc. Once it is time for you to receive income from the contract, the insurance company will pay you a certain income based on whatever your contract's value is at the time payments begin. In addition, all earnings will be subject to ordinary income tax.

Fixed

A traditional fixed annuity is fairly straightforward.[39]
You purchase a contract with an interest earnings rate that is fixed for a guaranteed period of time. When you are ready to retire you can move the monies from a fixed annuity to an immediate annuity where the insurance company will make regular income payments to you. Those payments will continue for the rest of your life and, if you choose, for the remainder of your spouse's life.

Fixed annuities don't typically offer significant upside potential, but many people like them for their guarantees, as well as for their predictability. Unlike variable annuities, which are subject to market risk and might be up one year and down the next, you lock into a fixed return for a specific period of time—more like CD rates but with deferred taxes on the earnings.

Fixed Index

To recap, variable annuities take on more risk to offer more possibilities to grow. Fixed annuities have less potential growth, but they protect your principal. [40]In the last couple of decades, many insurance companies have retooled their product line to offer fixed index annuities, which are sort of midway between variable and fixed annuities on that risk/reward spectrum. Fixed index annuities offer greater growth potential than traditional fixed annuities but less than variable annuities. Unlike variable annuities, however, fixed index annuities are protected from downside market losses.

Fixed index annuities earn interest that is tied to an external market index. This means that instead of your contract value growing at a set interest rate like a traditional fixed annuity, it has the potential to grow within a range. Your contract's value is credited interest based on the performance of an external market index such as the S&P 500. You don't invest in the S&P 500 directly, but each year, your annuity has the potential to earn interest based on the chosen index's performance, subject to caps and participation rates.

The way a cap works is that the insurance company allows you to participate in the growth of an index, but sets a cap on the maximum you could earn if the index goes up. For example: if your contract caps your interest at 7 percent and the index gains 35 percent in a year, your contract value increases 7 percent. If the index increases by 5 percent, your contract value gets the full 5 percent bump.

But since your money isn't actually invested in the market with a fixed index annuity, if the market nosedives (such as happened during 2000, 2008, 2020, and 2022, anyone?), you won't see any decrease in your contract value. Thus, no matter how badly the market performs, as long as you follow the terms of the contract, you won't lose any of the interest you were credited in previous years. So, if the S&P 500 shows a market loss of 30 percent one year, your contract value isn't going anywhere.

(In the interest of transparency, let's note that fees associated with riders *can* reduce your contract value even in years when a market decline has no adverse effect on the value.)

For those who are more interested in protection than growth potential, fixed index annuities can be an attractive option because, when the stock market has a long period of positive performance, a fixed index annuity can enjoy conservative growth. And during stretches where the market is erratic and stock values take significant losses, fixed index annuities won't lose anything due to the stock market volatility.

We often utilize FIAs during a client's working years when they have the majority of assets tied up in a retirement plan such as a 401(k) or IRA. As they get closer to retirement and don't want to risk a loss in their retirement savings, an FIA allows them an upside of potential returns, but also protects the assets from a market correction. In addition, for those looking for guaranteed income that they can't outlive, we will add a Minimum Withdrawal Benefit (MWB) rider to guarantee a payout percentage in the future that can help cover their fixed expenses.

Other Things to Know About Annuities

We just talked about the four kinds of annuity contracts available, but all of them have some commonalities as annuities.

For all annuities, the contractual guarantees are only as strong as the insurance company that sells the product, which makes it important to thoroughly check the credit ratings of any company whose products you are considering.[41]

Annuities are tax-deferred, meaning you don't have to pay taxes on interest earnings each year as the contract value grows. Instead, you will pay ordinary income taxes on your withdrawals. Annuities follow many of the rules of qualified retirement plans and are meant to be long-term products. Like other tax-deferred or tax-advantaged products, if you begin taking withdrawals from your contract before age fifty-nine-and-one-half, you may also have to pay a 10 percent federal penalty. Also, while annuities are generally considered illiquid, most contracts allow you to withdraw up to 10 percent of your contract value every year without any penalties. Withdraw any more, however, and you could incur additional surrender penalties.

Keep in mind, your withdrawals will deplete the accumulated cash value, death benefit, and possibly the rider values of your contract.

We believe that a properly structured annuity has a place within a retirement plan as it can perform several functions:

- Provide a steady income stream in retirement that can last for the life of two spouses.

- Limit downside losses as clients near retirement.
- Fund future fixed expenses in retirement so that other assets can be more aggressively invested.
- Provide income that can help an annuitant pay the taxes on RMDs, then use the remaining balance of the distribution to fund life insurance that will pass on a tax-free benefit to the next generation.
- Provide an investment option with upside potential and limit the downside risk.
- Reinsure a charitable gift annuity(s). A philanthropic person can donate money to a charity that in turn promises to pay out income to the donor. The charity can purchase a commercial annuity to reinsure its obligations, paying the donor a fixed amount each year for life. If reinsured, the charity keeps the remaining cash that doesn't go towards the purchase price of the annuity. The bottom line to the donor: You can do well by doing good.

Annuities aren't for everyone, but it's important to understand them before saying "yea" or "nay" on whether they fit into your plan; otherwise, you're not operating with complete information, wouldn't you agree? Regardless, you should talk to a financial advisor who can help you understand annuities, help you dissect your particular financial needs, and help show you whether an annuity is appropriate for your financial program.

CHAPTER 6

Social Security

S ocial Security is often the foundation of retirement income. Backed by the strength of the U.S. Treasury, it provides perhaps the most dependable paycheck you will have in retirement.

From the time you collect your first paycheck from the job that made you a bonafide taxpayer, you are paying into the grand old Social Security system. What grew and developed out of the pressures of the Great Depression has become one of the most popular government programs in the country, and, if you pay in for the equivalent of ten years or more, you too can benefit from the Social Security program.

Now, before we get into the nitty-gritty of Social Security, we'd like to address a current concern: Will Social Security still be there for you when you reach retirement age?

The Future of Social Security

This question is ever-present as headlines trumpet an underfunded Social Security program, alongside the sea of baby boomers retiring in droves and the comparatively smaller pool of younger people who are funding the system.

The Social Security Administration itself acknowledges this concern as each Social Security statement now contains a link to its website (ssa.gov) and a page entitled, "Will Social Security Be There For Me?"

Just a reminder, as if you needed one, that nothing in life is guaranteed. Additionally, depending on who you're listening to, Social Security funds may run low before 2034 thanks to the financial instability and government spending that accompanied the 2020 COVID-19 pandemic.

Before you get too discouraged, though, here are a few thoughts to keep you going:

- Even if the program is only paying 78 cents on the dollar for scheduled benefits, 78 percent is notably not zero.
- The Social Security Administration has made changes in the past to protect the fund's solvency, including increasing retirement ages and striking certain filing strategies.
- There are many changes Congress could make, and lawmakers routinely discuss how to fix the system, such as further increasing full retirement age and eligibility.
- One thing no one is seriously discussing is reneging on current obligations to retirees or the soon-to-retire.

Take heart. In our opinion, the real answer to the question, "Will Social Security be there for me?" is still yes.[42]

This question is important to consider when you look at how much we, as a nation, rely on this program. Did you know Social Security benefits replace about 40 percent of a person's original income when they retire?[43]

If you ask us, that's a pretty significant piece of one's retirement income puzzle.

Another caveat: You may not realize this, but no one can legally "advise" you about your Social Security benefits.

"But, Aviva, Andrew, isn't that part of what you do?" you may be asking. "And what about that nice gentleman at the Social Security Administration office I spoke with on the phone?"

Don't get us wrong. Social Security Administration employees know their stuff. They are trained to understand policies and programs, and they are usually pretty quick to tell you what you can and cannot do. But the government specifically stipulates, because Social Security is a benefit you alone have paid into and earned, your Social Security decisions are yours alone.

When it comes to financial advisors, we can't push you in any direction, but—and there's a big "but" here—working with a well-informed financial advisor is still incredibly handy for your Social Security decisions. Why? Because someone who's worth his or her salt will know what withdrawal strategies might pertain to your specific situation and will ask questions that can help you determine what you are looking for when it comes to your Social Security.

For instance, some people want the highest possible monthly benefit. Others want to start their benefits early, not always because of financial need. We heard about one man who called in to start his Social Security payments the day he qualified, just because he liked to think of it as the government paying back a debt it owed him, and he enjoyed the feeling of receiving a check from Uncle Sam.

Whatever your reasons, questions, or feelings regarding Social Security, the decision is yours alone. Working with a financial advisor can help you understand your options. An advisor can provide industry knowledge and use proprietary software or planning processes to analyze factors related to Social Security and how these benefits fit into your overall strategy for retirement income.

Full Retirement Age

When it comes to Social Security, it seems like many people don't fully understand the details. They don't take the time to understand the various options available. Instead, because it is common knowledge you can begin your benefits at age sixty-two, that's what many of us do. While more people are opting to delay taking benefits, age sixty-two is still firmly the most popular age to start.[44]

What many people fail to understand, however, is that by starting benefits early, they may be leaving a lot of money on the table. You see, the Social Security Administration bases your monthly benefit on two factors: your earnings history and your full retirement age (FRA).

From your earnings history, they pull the thirty-five years you made the most money and use a mathematical indexing formula to figure out a monthly average from those years. If you paid into the system for less than thirty-five years, then every year you didn't pay in will be counted as a zero.

Once they have calculated what your monthly earnings would be at FRA, the government then calculates what to put on your check based on how close you are to FRA. FRA was originally set at sixty-five, but, as the population aged and lifespans lengthened, the government shifted FRA later and later, based on an individual's year of birth. Check out the following chart to see when you will reach FRA.[45]

Age to Receive Full Social Security Benefits*	
(Called "full retirement age" [FRA] or "normal retirement age.")	
Year of Birth*	FRA
1937 or earlier	65
1938	65 and 2 months
1939	65 and 4 months
1940	65 and 6 months
1941	65 and 8 months
1942	65 and 10 months
1943-1954	66
1955	66 and 2 months
1956	66 and 4 months
1957	66 and 6 months
1958	66 and 8 months
1959	66 and 10 months
1960 and later	67
*If you were born on Jan. 1 of any year, you should refer to the previous year. (If you were born on the 1st of the month, we figure your benefit [and your full retirement age] as if your birthday was in the previous month.)	

When you reach FRA, you are eligible to receive 100 percent of whatever the Social Security Administration says is your full monthly benefit.

As noted previously, a person with a qualifying work history can begin receiving Social Security benefits starting at age sixty-two. But, for every year you claim benefits before reaching your FRA, your monthly check is reduced by 5 percent or more. Conversely, for every year you delay taking benefits past FRA, your monthly benefit increases by 8 percent until age seventy. After that, there is no monetary advantage to delaying Social Security benefits. While your circumstances and needs may vary, a lot of financial advisors still urge people to at least consider delaying until they reach age seventy.

Why wait?[46]

Taking benefits early could affect your monthly check by _____.								
62	63	64	65	FRA 66	67	68	69	70
-25 %	-20 %	-13.3 %	-6.7 %	0	+8 %	+16 %	+24 %	+32 %

Our philosophy is that if one member of a couple is still working and there isn't a need for supplemental income, we often suggest deferring taking Social Security until age seventy.

My Social Security

If you are over age thirty, you have probably received a notice from the Social Security Administration telling you to activate something called "My Social Security." This is a handy way to learn more about your particular benefit options, keep track of your earnings record, and calculate the benefits you have accrued over the years.

Essentially, My Social Security is an online account you can activate to see what your personal Social Security picture looks like. You can find this at www.ssa.gov/myaccount. This can be extremely helpful when it comes to planning for income in retirement and figuring out the difference between your anticipated income versus anticipated expenses.

My Social Security is also helpful because it's a great way to see if there is a problem. For instance, we have heard of one woman who, through diligently checking her tax records against her Social Security profile, discovered her Social Security check was shortchanging her, based on her earnings history. After taking the discrepancy to the Social Security Administration, they sent her what they owed her in makeup benefits.

COLA

Social Security is a largely guaranteed piece of the retirement puzzle: If you get a statement that says you should expect $1,000 a month, you can be sure you will receive $1,000 a month. But there is one variable: the cost-of-living adjustment, or COLA.

The COLA is an increase in your monthly check meant to address inflation in everyday life. After all, your expenses will likely continue to experience inflation in retirement, but you will no longer have the opportunity for the raises, bonuses, or promotions you had when you were working. Instead, your Social Security benefit receives an annual cost-of-living increase tied to the Department of Labor's Consumer Price Index for Urban Wage Earners and Clerical Workers, or CPI-W. If the CPI-W measurement shows inflation rose a certain amount for regular goods and services, then Social Security recipients will see that reflected in their COLA.

COLA adjustments have climbed as high as 14.3 percent (1980) and in 2023 reached 8.7 percent, the largest increase in more than forty years. But in a no- or low-inflation environment, such as in 2010, 2011, and 2016, Social Security recipients will not receive an adjustment.[47] Some view the COLA as a perk, bump, or bonus, but in reality, it works more like this: Your mom sends you to the store with $2.50 for a gallon of milk. Milk costs exactly $2.50. The next week, you go back with that same amount, but it is now $2.52 for a gallon, so you go back to Mom, and she gives you 2 cents. You aren't bringing home more milk—it just costs more money.

So, the COLA is less about "making more money" and more about keeping seniors' purchasing power from eroding when inflation is a big factor.

Spousal Benefits

We've talked about FRA, but another big Social Security decision involves spousal benefits.

If you or your spouse has a long stretch of zeros in your earnings history—perhaps if one of you stayed home for years, caring for children or sick relatives—you may want to consider filing for spousal benefits instead of filing on your own earnings history. A spousal benefit can be up to 50 percent of the primary wage earner's benefit at full retirement age.

To begin drawing a spousal benefit, you must be at least sixty-two years old, and the primary wage earner must have already filed for his or her benefit. While there are penalties for taking spousal benefits early, you cannot earn credits for delaying past full retirement age.[48]

As noted above, the spousal benefit can be a big deal for those who don't have a very long pay history, but it's important to weigh your own earned benefits against the option of withdrawing based upon a fraction of your spouse's benefits.

Let's say Peter's benefit at FRA, in his case sixty-seven, would be $1,600. If Peter begins his benefits right now, four years before FRA, his monthly check will be reduced to

$1,200. If Mary Jane begins taking spousal benefits in two years at the earliest date possible, her monthly benefits will be reduced by 67.5 percent, to $520 per month. (Remember, at FRA, the most she can qualify for is half of Peter's FRA benefit).

What if Peter and Mary Jane both wait until FRA? At sixty-seven, Peter begins taking his full benefit of $1,600 a month. Two years later, when she reaches age sixty-seven, Mary Jane will qualify for $800 a month. By waiting until FRA, the couple's monthly benefit goes from $1,720 to $2,400.

What if Peter delays until age seventy to get his maximum possible benefit? For each year he delays past FRA, his monthly benefit increases by 8 percent. This means, at seventy, he could file for a monthly benefit of $2,015. However, delayed retirement credits do not affect spousal benefits, so as soon as Peter files at seventy, Mary Jane would also file (at age sixty-eight) for her maximum benefit of $800, so their highest possible combined monthly check is $2,815.[49]

When it comes to your Social Security benefits, you obviously will want to consider whether a monthly check based on a fraction of your spouse's earnings will be comparable to or larger than your own earnings history.

Divorced Spouses

There are a few considerations for those who have gone through a divorce. If you 1) were married for ten years or more and 2) have since been divorced for at least two years and 3) are unmarried and 4) your ex-spouse qualifies to begin Social Security, you will qualify for a spousal benefit based on your ex-husband or ex-wife's earnings history at FRA. A divorced spousal benefit is different from the married spousal benefit in one way: You don't have to wait for your ex-spouse to file before you can file yourself.[50]

For instance, Charles and Moira were married for fifteen years before their divorce, when he was thirty-six and she was forty. Moira has been remarried for twenty years, and, although Charles briefly remarried, his second marriage ended after a few years. Charles' benefits are largely calculated based on his many years of volunteering in schools, meaning his personal monthly benefit is close to zero.

Although Moira has deferred her retirement, opting to delay benefits until she is seventy, Charles can begin taking benefits calculated from Moira's work history at FRA as early as sixty-two. However, he will also have the option of waiting until FRA to collect the maximum, or 50 percent of Moira's earned monthly benefit at her FRA.

Widowed Spouses

If your marriage ended with the death of your spouse, you might claim a benefit for your spouse's earned income as his or her widow/widower, called a survivor's benefit. Unlike a spousal benefit or divorced benefits, if your husband or wife dies, you can claim his or her full benefit. Also, unlike spousal benefits, if you need to, you can begin taking income when you turn sixty. However, as with other early benefit options, your monthly check will be permanently reduced for withdrawing benefits before FRA.

If your spouse began taking benefits before he or she died, you can't delay withdrawing your survivor's benefits to get delayed credits. The Social Security Administration maintains you can only get as much from a survivor's benefit as your deceased spouse might have received had he or she lived.[51]

Taxes, Taxes, Taxes

With Social Security, as with everything, it is important to consider taxes. It may be surprising, but your Social Security benefits are not tax-free. Despite having been taxed to accrue

76

those benefits in the first place, you may have to pay Uncle Sam income taxes on up to 85 percent of your Social Security.

The Social Security Administration figures these taxes using what they call "the provisional income formula." Your provisional income formula differs from the adjusted gross income you use for your regular income taxes. Instead, to find out how much of your Social Security benefit is taxable, the Social Security Administration calculates it this way:

Provisional Income = Adjusted Gross Income + Nontaxable Interest + ½ of Social Security

See that piece about nontaxable interest? That generally means interest from government bonds and notes. It surprises many people that, although you may not pay taxes on those assets, their income will count against you when it comes to Social Security taxation.

Once you have figured out your provisional income (also called "combined income"), you can use the following chart to figure out your Social Security taxes.[52]

Taxes on Social Security		
Provisional Income = Adjusted Gross Income + Nontaxable Interest + ½ of Social Security		
If you are ____ and your provisional income is____, then...		Uncle Sam will tax ___ of your Social Security
Single	Married, filing jointly	
Less than $25,000	Less than $32,000	0%
$25,000 to $34,000	$32,000 to $44,000	Up to 50%
More than $34,000	More than $44,000	Up to 85%

This is one more reason it may benefit you to work with financial and tax professionals. They can look at your entire financial picture to make your overall retirement plan as tax-efficient as possible—including your Social Security benefit.

At Sapers & Wallack, we like to plan in advance for future taxation in retirement. One of the ways we do this is by looking at diversification of accounts by tax status—tax-deferred, taxable, and tax-free. By diversifying your accounts from a tax perspective, you can pick and choose what accounts you pull from to fund your lifestyle in retirement, potentially lowering your overall tax impact by not jumping into a higher marginal tax bracket.

We also advise clients about the consequences of working while taking Social Security before reaching your full retirement age. The full effect of this—a possible further reduction in your monthly benefit—is explained in the section below.

But let's note here that we typically recommend to avoid taking Social Security before reaching FRA unless you have serious health concerns or a family history of lower life expectancy. In this case, you may want to consider starting Social Security "early," even though that results in a permanent reduction in your monthly benefit. The idea of "getting a little something is better than nothing" makes some sense if you truly believe that you might not live long enough to see an enhanced Social Security benefit at age seventy. If, however, you reasonably hope to experience a normal life expectancy (or more), it is our recommendation to hold off starting Social Security until your benefits "max out" at age seventy.

Working and Social Security: The Earnings Test

If you haven't reached FRA, but you started your Social Security benefits and are still working, things get a little hairy.

Because you have started Social Security payments, the Social Security Administration will still pay out your benefits (at that reduced rate, of course, because you haven't reached your FRA). But, because you are working, the organization must also take regular FICA withholding—a.k.a., the Social Security tax we pay throughout our years of employment—from your paycheck. In other words, you will continue paying into the Social Security system even as you are taking money out of it! See how this complicates matters?

In another work-related issue, the government has what is called the "earnings test" under which it can reduce your benefit if you earn too much through employment while receiving Social Security prior to reaching FRA. For 2023, you can earn up to $21,240 in wages without affecting your Social Security check. But, for every $2 you earn over that amount, the Social Security Administration will withhold $1 from your regular benefit check.

On a more positive note, beginning in the month you reach FRA, and in future years after doing so, you are no longer subject to any earnings withholding. Keep in mind too, that the money the government withholds from your Social Security benefits while you are working before FRA will be tacked back onto your benefits check after FRA.[53]

Social Security is an integral part of the retirement plans of many people. As previously mentioned, we try to generate guaranteed income streams in retirement, and one of those pillars is Social Security. Though it is not intended to cover all your retirement expenses, it should help in covering a baseline of fixed expenses for your family.

We look at each client's individual and personalized needs when advising on when to begin taking Social Security from ages sixty-two to seventy. Again, the decision is unique to each client, but if possible, we like to wait on taking distributions as higher monthly payments will certainly help in the later years of your lifetime.

CHAPTER 7
Taxes

W here to begin with taxes? Perhaps by acknowledging we all bear responsibility for the resources we share. Roads, bridges, schools . . . It is the patriotic duty of every American to pay their fair share of taxes. Many would agree with this sentiment. However, while they don't mind paying their fair share, they're not interested in paying one cent more than that!

Now, just talking taxes probably takes your mind to April—tax season. You are probably thinking about all the forms you collect and how you file. Perhaps you are thinking about your certified public accountant or another qualified tax professional and saying to yourself, "I've already got taxes taken care of, thanks!"

However, what we see when people come into our office is that their relationship with their tax professional is purely a January through April relationship. That means they may have a tax professional, but not a tax *planner.*

We believe tax planning extends beyond filing taxes. In April, we are required to settle our accounts with the IRS to make sure we have paid up on our bill, or to even the score if we have overpaid. But real tax planning is about making each financial move in a way that allows you to keep the most money in your pocket and out of Uncle Sam's.

Now, as a caveat, we want to emphasize we are neither CPAs nor tax planners, but we see the way taxes affect our clients, and we have plenty of experience helping clients implement tax-efficient strategies in their retirement plans in conjunction with their tax professionals.

Part of our process involves helping clients who've not yet built a relationship with a tax planner. Over the years, we've developed multiple working relationships with CPAs, tax advisors, and estate attorneys whose services we recommend to clients who might not otherwise encounter these additional layers of professional help.

That's because CPAs and lawyers, in our opinion, are not the most pro-active group of advisors! They seldom, if ever, reach out to people on a whim or check in to see if anything has changed in their clients' lives. Instead, they wait to be called. This isn't to say, mind you, that there aren't some very qualified CPAs and lawyers out there; we wouldn't work with them if they weren't competent. But having established that and understanding how many of these professionals operate, we have often had to be the pro-active ones quarterbacking much of the tax planning that is needed.

Most strategic partnerships we develop do more than shuttle business back and forth. Rather, we work to develop good teamwork relationships in which we trust the judgment and skills of the professionals we consult outside of our office. We often educate our strategic partners on concepts we have used successfully so that when they are faced with a similar situation, they will know to consider these options or bring us in to help solve their clients' problems. Our best strategic partners are those who don't believe they have every answer, but instead enjoy working together with us to find ways to improve the lives of the clients we might share.

It is especially important to us to help our clients develop tax-efficient strategies in their financial plans as each dollar they can keep in their pockets is a dollar we can put to work for them.

Moreover, each dollar saved from taxes is one that can be passed most efficiently to loved ones. We'll examine in more detail the tax obligation on inherited money in a later chapter, but for now, let's just note that there are typically three beneficiaries of your estate: family, charity, and the IRS. And without tax planning, the IRS can be the largest beneficiary of the money you worked hard to earn.

There are headlines in the financial news almost every day about a well-known person who died without a will or proper planning. The artist still known as Prince (as we will forever remember him) had over $100 million in assets, and almost as many people fighting over who would receive those assets. The IRS was at the head of the line.

There are so many great strategies to ensure that the money you leave behind gets to the people or charities you want to have it. It's our goal, both in our daily operations and in this book, to at least make you aware of these tax-saving options.

In this chapter, we'll talk about using tax-free vehicles—the Roth IRA being foremost among them—as a way of passing tax-free money to beneficiaries. We'll talk in another chapter about the tax-free nature of life insurance benefits. In yet another chapter, we'll discuss using a will or trust as a way in which you can name charities as beneficiaries and avoid any of your estate being used to pay taxes. We'll also talk later about the role of an irrevocable trust as a means of blunting estate taxes.

For now, however, let's look at the impact of taxes in our financial lives—both now and in the future—and how tax planning can affect how much of your money stays in your pocket.

The Federal Debt

In the United States, taxes can be a rather uncertain proposition. Depending on who is in the White House and which party controls Congress, we might be tempted to assume tax rates could either decline or increase accordingly in the next four to eight years. However, there is one (large!) factor we, as a nation, must confront: the national debt.

Currently, according to USDebtClock.org, we are over $32.5 trillion in debt and climbing. That's $32 and a half *trillion* with a "T." With just $1 trillion, you could park it in the bank at a zero percent interest rate and spend more than $54 million every day for fifty years without hitting a zero balance.

Even if Congress got a handle on that debt and stopped it from its daily compounding, divided by each taxpayer, we each would owe about $246,000. So, will that be check, cash, or Venmo?[54]

Our point here isn't to give you anxiety. We're just cautioning you that even with the rosiest of outlooks on our personal income tax rates, none of us should count on low tax rates for the long term. Instead, you and your network of professionals (tax, legal, and financial) should constantly be looking for ways to take advantage of tax-saving opportunities as they come. After all, the best "luck" is when proper planning meets opportunity.

So, how can we get started?

Know Your Limits

One of the foundational pieces of tax planning is knowing what tax bracket you are in, based on your income after subtracting pre-tax or untaxed assets. Your income taxes are based on your taxable income.

One reason to know your taxable income and your income tax rate is so you can see how far away you are from the next lower or higher tax bracket. This is particularly important when it comes to decisions such as gifting and Roth IRA conversions.

For instance, taking information from the 2022 federal income tax return they filed in 2023, Mallory and Ralph's taxable income was just over $345,000, putting them in the

32 percent tax bracket and about $4,900 above the upper end of the 24 percent tax bracket. They have already maxed out their retirement funds' tax-exempt contributions for the year. Their daughter, Gloria, is a sophomore in college. This couple could shave a considerable amount off their tax bill if they use the $4,900 to help Gloria out with groceries and school—something they were likely to do anyway, but now can be done deliberately as part of an overall financial strategy that could move our mythical couple down into a lower tax bracket.

We use Mallory and Ralph only as an example—your circumstances are probably different—but we think this nicely illustrates the way planning ahead for taxes can save you money.

Lower Taxes in Retirement? Really?

Many people anticipate being in a lower tax bracket in retirement. It makes sense: You won't be earning a salary, but you also won't need to earn additional income to pay for all those work-related expenses—work clothes, transportation, lunch meetings, etc.

Yet, do you really plan on changing your lifestyle after retirement? Do you plan to cut down on the number of times you eat out, scale back vacations, skimp on travel? If not, you are going to need income—perhaps the same income level you knew during your working years—and much of that will likely be taxable income.

What we see in our office is many couples actually spending *more* in the first few years, or maybe the first decade, of retirement. Sure, that may taper off later on, but usually just in time for their budget to be hit with greater health and long-term care expenses.

Do you see where this is going? Many people plan as though their taxable income will be lower in retirement and are surprised when the tax bills come in and look more or less the same as they used to. It's better to plan for the worst and hope for the best, wouldn't you agree?

Tax-deferred accounts

One sometimes-unexpected piece of tax planning in retirement concerns your 401(k) or IRA. Most of us have one of these accounts or an equivalent. Throughout our working years, we dutifully pay in a portion of our earnings in these tax-deferred accounts. And there's the rub: tax-deferred, not tax-free. The tax impact of those 401(k)s and IRAs is about to be felt in retirement. The taxes the government deferred when you were in your working years are now coming due as you withdraw money from those accounts—often as a source of retirement income—and you will pay taxes on that income at whatever your current tax rate is.

Just to ensure Uncle Sam gets his due, the government also has a required minimum distribution, or RMD, rule. Beginning at age seventy-three (for those who reach age seventy-two after January 1, 2023), you are required to withdraw a certain minimum amount every year from your 401(k) or IRAs. A failure to do so will incur a tax penalty on any RMD you should have withdrawn but didn't—and that's on top of the income tax you will pay on the distribution you do take. The SECURE Act 2.0 reduced the penalty to 25 percent (from 50 percent previously). Timely corrections can further reduce the penalty to 10 percent.[55]

Now let's consider the more tax-friendly nature of the Roth IRA, the use of which constitutes a tax strategy we are happy to discuss with clients wanting to learn more about reducing taxes in retirement.

Think of the difference between a Roth and a traditional retirement account as the difference between taxing the seed versus taxing the harvest. Because Roths are funded with post-tax dollars, there are no tax penalties for early

86

withdrawals of the principal, nor are there taxes on the growth of the account after you reach age fifty-nine-and-one-half. Perhaps best of all, there are no RMDs. (But let's note here that you must own a Roth account for a minimum of five years before you are able to take advantage of all its features.)

This is one more area where it pays to be aware of your tax bracket. Some people may find it advantageous to "convert" their traditional tax-deferred retirement accounts to Roth accounts in a year in which they are in a lower tax bracket. Others may opt to put any excess RMDs from their traditional retirement accounts into other products, like stocks or insurance.

Does all of this make your head spin? Understandable. That's why we'll devote the entire next chapter to explaining these concepts in even greater detail. It's also why it's so important to work with a financial advisor and tax planner who can help you execute these sorts of tax-efficient strategies and help you understand what you are doing and why.

If you are philanthropically inclined, you can also opt for a Zero Estate Tax strategy and pay nothing to the federal government. At the same time, you can make an impact by supporting some worthwhile causes and still providing for your family. All it takes is some good planning.

CHAPTER 8

401(k)s & IRAs

H ave you heard? Today's retirement is not your parents' retirement. You see, back in the day, it was pretty common to work for one company for the vast majority of your career and then retire with a gold watch and a pension.

The gold watch was a symbol of the quality time you had put in at that company, but the pension was more than a symbol. Instead, it was a guarantee—as solid as your employer—that they would show appreciation for your hard work with a certain amount of income in retirement. Did you see the caveat there? Your pension's guarantee was *as solid as your employer.* The problem was, what if your employer went under?

Companies that failed couldn't pay their retired employees' pensions, leading to financial challenges for many. Beginning in 1974 with Congress' passage of the Employee Retirement Income Security Act, federal legislation and regulations aimed at protecting retirees were everywhere. One piece of legislation included a relatively obscure section of the Internal Revenue Code, added in 1978. Section 401(k), to be specific.

IRC section 401, subsection k, created tax advantages for employer-sponsored financial plans, even if the main contributor was the employee. Over the years, more employers took note, beginning an age of transition away from pensions and toward 401(k) plans—a retirement account with certain tax benefits and restrictions on the investments or other financial products inside of it.

Essentially, 401(k)s and their individual retirement account (IRA) counterparts are "wrappers" that provide tax benefits around assets; typically, the assets that compose IRAs and 401(k)s are mutual funds, stock and bonds, and money market accounts. These days, some companies are also offering different kinds of annuity options within their plans.

Where pensions are defined-*benefit* plans, 401(k)s and IRAs are defined-*contribution* plans. The one-word change outlines the basic difference. Pensions spell out what benefit you can expect to receive from the plan at retirement but not how much money it will take to fund those benefits. With 401(k)s, an employer sets a standard for how much they will contribute (if any), and you get to decide how much you want to contribute. In these plans you define what goes in but don't know exactly what will come out at retirement.

Modern employment looks very different than it did when the defined-benefit pension system was more prominent. A 2020 survey by the Bureau of Labor Statistics found that U.S. workers stayed with their employers a median of 4.1 years. Workers ages fifty-five to sixty-four had a little more staying power and were most likely to stay with their employer for about ten years.[56] Participation in 401(k) plans has steadily risen this century, totaling $7.3 trillion in assets in 2021 compared to $3.1 trillion in 2011. About 60 million active participants engaged in 401(k) plans in 2020.[57]

Those statistics make it clear that 401(k) plans have replaced pensions at many companies and, for that matter, the gold watch.

A Shift in Risk

One effect of the transition from traditional pension plans to defined contribution plans is a shift in risk from that borne by the employer to that put on the employee.

The defined contribution plan, quite frankly, creates a very different retirement picture than its predecessor presented. A 401(k), for example, brings market risk directly into the picture and makes you, the employee, assume all that risk. You invest money directly from your paycheck—an amount you determine within contribution limits established by the IRS—on a pre-tax basis. You also decide how that money will be invested through choices generally offered by the financial services company that manages the plan for your employer. The value of your account goes up and down as the market does, and whatever balance remains is yours to spend down in retirement.

Contrast this to a defined benefit plan in which the employer takes on all risk. In a pension plan, the employer contributes monthly with the promise that when you retire, they will provide a percentage of your three highest earning years for the remainder of your life. The employer hopes that market performance will produce returns that will allow them to meet their pension obligations. But if the markets do not cooperate and go down, it is on the employer to make up the difference.

If there is anything to learn from this paradigm shift, it's that you must look out for yourself. Whether you have worked for a company for two years or twenty, you are still the one who has to look out for your own best interests. That holds doubly true when it comes to preparing for retirement. If you are one of the lucky ones who still has a pension, good for you. But for the rest of us, it is likely that a 401(k)—or possibly one of its nonprofit- or government-sector counterparts, a 403(b) or 457 or Thrift Savings Plan—is one of your biggest assets for retirement.

Some employers offer incentives to contribute to their company plans, like a company match. On that subject, we have one thing to say: *Do it!* Nothing in life is free, as they say, but a company match on your retirement funds is about as close to free money as it gets. If you can make the minimum to qualify for your company's match at all, go for it.

Now, it's likely, during our working years, we mostly "set and forget" our 401(k) funding. Because it is tax-advantaged, your employer is taking money from your paycheck—before taxes—and putting it into your plan for you. Maybe you got to pick a selection of investments, or maybe you chose to invest in a target date fund. Either way, while you are gainfully employed, your most impactful decision may just be to fund your plan in the first place. But, when you are ready to retire or move jobs, you have choices to make that require a little more thought and care.

When you are ready to part ways with your job, you have a few options:

- Leave the money where it is
- Take the cash (and pay income taxes and perhaps a 10 percent additional penalty tax if you are younger than age fifty-nine-and-one-half)
- Transfer the money to another employer plan (if the new plan allows)
- Roll the money over into a self-directed IRA

These are just general options. You will have to decide, hopefully with the help of a financial advisor, what's right for you. Leaving the money where it is may not be an option; if the account value is small, some companies have direct cash payout or rollover policies that limit your options once someone is no longer employed.

Given how often the current generations change jobs these days, you likely have a 401(k) with your current company, but you may also have a string of retirement accounts trailing you from other jobs.

It's not unheard of for people who switch jobs frequently to lose track of the funds they have in old 401(k) plans. One client of ours, for example, told us she had four old 401(k) plans, but when we started researching, we realized she actually had *six* accounts spread out among different institutions. Moreover, some small balances in her older plans had been transferred into an IRA that had been sitting in cash for decades with almost no growth. This could have been a major problem when she turned seventy-three and had to begin taking RMDs from accounts she had completely forgotten about.

To repeat a point made earlier, but one important enough to mention yet again: The IRS assesses a 25 percent penalty for every dollar you should have taken in required distributions but didn't. (This penalty, by the way, was reduced by the SECURE Act 2.0 from the previous 50 percent fine; who says your government doesn't love you?) And believe us, the IRS doesn't care that you forgot about this money, or that the dog ate your paperwork, or any other excuse you might offer for not taking the correct distribution.

When it comes to your retirement income, it's important to be able to pull together *all* your assets, so you can examine what you have and where, and then decide what you will do with it.

Tax-Qualified, Tax-Preferred, Tax-Deferred … Still TAXED

Financial media often cite IRAs and 401(k)s for their tax benefits. With these traditional plans, you put your money in on a pre-tax basis, and it hopefully grows—still untaxed—for years, even decades. That's why these accounts are called "tax-qualified" or "tax-deferred" assets. But they aren't tax-free!

Rarely does Uncle Sam allow business to continue without receiving his piece of the pie, and your retirement assets are no different. If you didn't pay taxes on the front end, you will pay taxes on the back end when you withdraw money from these accounts in retirement. This isn't an inherently good or bad thing; it's just the way it is. It's important to understand, though, for the sake of planning ahead.

In retirement, many people assume they will be in a lower tax bracket. But ask yourself this: Are you planning to pare down your lifestyle in retirement? Perhaps you are, and perhaps you will have substantially less need for income in retirement. But many of our clients tell us they want to live life more or less the same as they always have. The money they would previously have spent on business attire or gas for their commute they now want to spend on hobbies, travel and grandchildren. That's all fine, and it is doable for many of them. But does it put them in a lower tax bracket? Probably not.

Keep in mind, IRAs, 401(k)s, and their alternatives have a few limitations because of their special tax status. For one thing, the IRS sets limits on your contributions to these retirement accounts. If you are contributing to a 401(k) or an equivalent nonprofit or government plan, your annual contribution limit is $22,500 (as of 2023). If you are age fifty or older, the IRS allows additional contributions, called "catch-up contributions," of up to $7,500, raising the top total contribution limit to $30,000. For an IRA, the limit is $6,500, with a catch-up limit of an additional $1,000.[58] Beginning in 2024, catch-up contributions for individuals with income exceeding $145,000 must transfer into a Roth IRA.[59]

Because their tax advantages come from their intended use as retirement income, withdrawing funds from these accounts before you turn fifty-nine-and-one-half can carry stiff penalties. In addition to fees your investment management company might charge, you will have to pay income tax *and* a 10 percent federal tax penalty, with few exceptions.

The fifty-nine-and-one-half rule for retirement accounts is incredibly important to remember, especially when you're young. Younger workers are often tempted to cash out an IRA from a previous employer and then are surprised to find their checks missing 20 percent of the account value to income taxes, penalty taxes, and account fees.

Many millennials we see in our practice say, while they may be socking money away in their workplace retirement plan, it is often the *only* place they are saving. This could be problematic later because of the fifty-nine-and-one-half rule; what if you have an emergency? It is important to fund your retirement, but you also need to have some liquid assets handy as emergency funds. This can help you avoid breaking into your retirement accounts and incurring taxes and penalties because of the fifty-nine-and-one-half rule.

RMDs

Remember how we talked about the 401(k) or IRA being a "tax wrapper" for your funds? Well, eventually, Uncle Sam will want a bite of that candy bar. So, when you turn seventy-three, the government requires that you withdraw a portion of your account, which the IRS calculates based on the size of your account and your estimated lifespan. This required minimum distribution, or RMD, is the government's way of collecting taxes from your earnings. Because you didn't pay taxes on the front end, you will now pay income taxes on whatever you withdraw, including your RMDs.

Let us reiterate something we pointed out in the Longevity chapter. Once you reach RMD age, you will face a tax penalty on any RMD monies you should have withdrawn but didn't— and that's on top of income tax you will pay on the money you did withdraw. As we noted previously, the SECURE Act 2.0 reduced the penalty and raised the RMD age to seventy-three from seventy-two. It also stipulates the RMD age will increase to seventy-five for those turning seventy-four after December 31, 2032.)[60]

95

One additional note on RMDs. Even after you begin taking them, you can continue contributing to your 401(k) or IRAs if you are still employed, which can affect the whole discussion on RMDs and possible tax considerations.

If you don't need income from your retirement accounts, RMDs can seem like more of a tax burden than an income boon. While some people prefer to reinvest their RMDs, this comes with the possibility of additional taxation: You'll pay income taxes on your RMDs and then potential capital gains taxes on the growth of your investments. If you are legacy-minded, there are other ways to use RMDs, many of which have tax benefits.

SECURE Act 2.0 provisions

In addition to changes imposed for RMD ages, Secure Act 2.0 also expanded access to retirement savings using different methods. Provisions in the legislation go into effect at different times, ranging from 2023-25.

- Beginning January 2, 2024, plan participants can access up to $1,000 (once a year) from retirement savings for emergency personal or family expenses without paying a 10 percent early withdrawal penalty.
- Beginning January 2, 2024, employees can establish a Roth emergency savings account of up to $2,500 per participant.
- Beginning January 2, 2024, domestic abuse survivors can withdraw the lesser of $10,000 or 50 percent of their retirement account without penalty.
- Beginning January 1, 2023, victims of a qualified, federally declared disaster can withdraw up to $22,000 from their retirement account without penalty.[61]

Permanent Life Insurance

We mentioned previously that there are alternatives to reinvesting RMDs. One way is to turn them into a legacy gift through permanent life insurance. Often, people who don't need the RMDs as income may find that their kids will inherit more if they gift the RMDs to the kids as premiums on a life insurance policy that is removed from their estate. Assuming they can qualify medically for this coverage, a properly structured life insurance policy can pass on a sizable death benefit to your beneficiaries, income tax-free, as part of your general legacy plan.

ILIT

If you are interested in using your RMDs for legacy planning, and want to keep the proceeds estate tax free, you may want to work with an estate planning attorney to create an irrevocable life insurance trust (ILIT). This is basically a permanent life insurance policy placed within a trust. Because the trust is irrevocable, you would relinquish control of it, but unlike owning your own permanent life insurance policy, your death benefit won't count toward your taxable estate and thus the proceeds would be income and estate tax free.

Annuities

Because annuities can be tax-deferred, using all or a portion of your RMDs to fund an annuity contract can be a way to further delay taxation while guaranteeing your income payments (either to you or your loved ones) later. Of course, this assumes you don't need the RMD income during the early years of retirement.

Qualified Charitable Distributions

If you are charity-minded, you may gift RMDs to a charitable organization instead of using them for income. You must do this directly from your retirement account (you can't take the RMD check and then pay the charity) for your withdrawals to be qualified charitable distributions (QCDs), but this is one way of realizing some of the benefits of a charitable legacy during your own lifetime.

The advantage of doing this is that you will not have to pay income taxes on your QCDs, and they won't count toward your annual charitable tax deduction limit. In addition, you'll be able to see how the organization you are supporting uses your donations during your lifetime. You should consult a financial advisor on how to correctly make a QCD, particularly since the SECURE Act has implemented a few regulations on this point.[62]

The QCD is one of several strategies we look at when trying to minimize tax consequences of RMDs. Another is the **Roth IRA conversion**.[63] These are done most typically in the early years of retirement when people often find themselves in a lower tax bracket before they begin taking Social Security. Such a time can be a prime opportunity for a Roth conversion, so let's look at this concept more closely.

Roth IRA

Since the Taxpayer Relief Act of 1997, there has been a different kind of retirement account, or "tax wrapper," available to the public: the Roth. Roth IRAs, Roth 401(k)s and Roth 403(b)s each differ from their traditional counterparts in one big way: You pay your taxes up front. This means, once your post-tax money is in the Roth account, as long as you follow the rules and limitations of that account, your future distributions are truly tax-free. You won't pay income tax when you take withdrawals, so, in turn, you don't have to worry about RMDs. However, Roth accounts have the same limitations as traditional 401(k)s and IRAs when it comes to withdrawing money before age fifty-nine-and-one-half, with the added stipulation that the account must have been open for at least five years in order for the account holder to make withdrawals.

We frequently do Roth conversions—the process of moving money out of a tax-deferred account and putting the after-tax remainder into a Roth—for our clients as they are allowed at most any time. However, it is advisable to plan for them in advance as the best time to do them is when you are in a lower tax bracket or have tax losses that could offset the income tax you will owe whenever you more money out of a traditional IRA or 401(k).

A prime example of a Roth conversion candidate would be someone who retires at age sixty-five but wants to delay Social Security until age seventy. During the years from sixty-five to seventy, their earned income could be lower and their taxable income may be minimal, especially if they can live off tax-advantaged dividends, or—better yet—tax-free distributions from a Roth IRA. A person or couple in this situation might be able to convert money from a traditional IRA to a Roth account at just a 12 percent tax rate until their taxable income reaches the $89,450 threshold for the 22 percent tax bracket (based on 2023 marginal tax rates for a married couple filing jointly).

Keep in mind that Roth *conversions* are not allowed after RMDs begin. The price of moving money out of your qualified retirement accounts—whether you actually need that money or not—suddenly got higher.

Taking Charge

As mentioned earlier, the 401(k) and IRA have largely replaced pensions, but they aren't an equal trade.

Pensions are employer-funded; the money feeding into them is money that wouldn't ever show up on your pay stub. Because 401(k)s are self-funded, you must actively and consciously save. This distinction has made a difference when it comes to funding retirement. The "2023 Planning and Progress Study" by Northwestern Mutual reported that

American adults surveyed said they anticipated needing a retirement "nest egg" of at least $1.27 million in order to retire comfortably. In contrast, the report said the average American had saved only $89,300 for retirement. (Perhaps it qualifies as good news that this figure is up 3 percent from the $86,869 savings figure reported in 2022.)[64]

There can be many reasons why people underfund their retirement plans, like being overwhelmed by the investment choices, don't think they can afford it, or taking withdrawals from their 401(k)s when they leave an employer. Still, the reason at the top of the list is this: People simply aren't participating to begin with.

So, whether you use a 401(k) with an employer or fund your own IRA separate from your workplace, the most important retirement savings decision you can make is to sock away money somewhere in the first place.

CHAPTER 9

Life Insurance

O ur clients are not typically gamblers, so it's understandable that life insurance fits somewhere in the financial plans for many of them. Life insurance, after all, is most often used to mitigate risk.

For example, people purchase it to replace the lost income of a breadwinner. Some use it to provide liquidity to pay estate taxes or to create a legacy for kids or charity. Others use it as a tax-advantaged investment vehicle.

Depending on the purpose and the timeline, it is important to consider which insurance product fits best in your specific situation, and so we'll examine various types of life insurance in this chapter.

Insurance: The Basics

If you haven't been casting around in the life insurance pond much, then let's take a second to cover the basics. During our working lives, we likely have some kind of basic term life policy, either privately or through our employers. Term life insurance protects an individual for a certain period of time—usually ten to thirty years. It typically correlates to a certain amount of wages (if it's an employer's plan) or a coverage amount chosen by the individual (if it's a person's private insurance).

At its most basic, term insurance provides funds for our loved ones and can be used for a number of purposes, including covering funeral expenses or much more. People often will take out enough to cover living expenses or replacement of lost income. The premium for a term life policy will be based on things like the amount of coverage, your age, your health, and the term of the policy. The calculation that determines the cost is a probability of your risk of dying that year (based on your age and health) multiplied by the amount of insurance you want. Nowadays, these policies are issued in ten, fifteen, twenty and thirty-year time horizons where the cost is averaged out over the time period and is guaranteed to stay flat for the years you purchased. The limitation of term insurance, however, is that while the price is fixed for the term of the contract, when that term is over, the coverage either gets extremely expensive or terminates.

The older you are, the more likely it is you will have health events or other issues that could make it more difficult to obtain life insurance, as well as make that coverage more expensive. Some consumers may see this as a disadvantage of term life insurance. They pay into a policy for twenty years, and then it reaches its "endowment"—the end of the contract term—and there are no additional benefits.

Having said this, let's also note that many term insurance policies today are convertible to permanent for some period of time so that if you become less healthy, you can "insure" your future insurability with the conversion feature.

Permanent Insurance

Aside from the basic term life policies many wage-earners hold, insurance companies also have permanent policies, also sometimes referred to as "cash value insurance." With a permanent insurance contract, your policy will typically remain in force as long as you continue to keep it funded.

(There is an exception for whole life policies, which we'll get to later.)

A permanent insurance contract has two pieces: the death benefit and cash value accumulation. Both are spelled out in your contract. As these products gained recognition, people began to realize how they had significant advantages when it came to taxes. We don't really want to get too technical, but it is really the technical details that make these policies even more valuable to their owners. For not only does the consumer receive an income-tax-free death benefit for their beneficiaries, but they may also be able to borrow against the cash value of their policy, also income-tax-free, if they end up needing the money.

For example, let's say Emma considers purchasing a life insurance policy when she's thirty. She hates the idea of not having anything to show for her premiums over ten to twenty years, so she decides to use a permanent policy. Then, when she's close to fifty, her brother finds himself in dire straits. Emma wants to help, and she's been a diligent saver. The catch is most of her money is in products like her 401(k) or an annuity. These may be fabulous products suitable for her needs, but her circumstances have changed, and she's looking for ways to help her sibling without incurring significant tax penalties.

This is where her permanent life insurance policy offers flexibility and options. She can borrow from the accumulated cash value in her policy, free of income taxes. So, let's say she borrows a few thousand dollars from her policy. She doesn't have to pay taxes on any of it, and she can pay it back into her policy at any time. Now let's say Emma dies before she "settles up" her policy (or pays back that loan). As long as she continued making premium payments or otherwise kept her policy adequately funded until she died, then her beneficiaries will still receive a death benefit, minus the outstanding policy loan.

Here are the central themes on properly structured permanent life insurance policies: tax-free death benefit and income-tax-free withdrawals through policy loans are available as long as the premiums continue to be paid; and a minimum rate of cash value accumulation that is guaranteed by the strength of the insurer.

Now, let's dive a little deeper into the two basic categories of permanent insurance: whole life policies and universal life policies.

Whole Life Insurance

With basic whole life, an actuary in a back office has calculated what a person your age with your intended death benefit coverage, your health history, your potential lifespan— and other minutiae—should pay. They then create a level or flat premium rate. Depending on how the insurer's rate tables are calculated, your whole life policy will "endow" at a certain age—ninety, one hundred, one hundred twenty, etc.—so there is the risk you could outlive the policy, in which case the death benefit would pay out to you instead of your beneficiaries. This could create unplanned tax consequences.

To qualify for your whole life policy, you will complete a medical questionnaire and possibly a paramedical exam. Then, based on that information, an underwriter will place you in one of these actuarial categories to determine your premium rate. One benefit of whole life insurance is the insurance company will credit a certain amount back into the policy's cash value based on your contract's guaranteed rate. Some insurance companies may also pay a dividend back to policyholders at the company's discretion.

Take Emma from the preceding example, and let's consider the scenario if her permanent insurance policy was a whole life policy. When she first purchased the contract, the insurance agent would have been able to tell her what her locked-in premium rate would be. She would pay the same amount, year after year, to keep her contract in force. And she could also calculate her policy's minimum cash value to the penny.

Universal Life Insurance

If whole life is the basic permanent life insurance policy, universal life is the souped-up model. It has (figuratively speaking) eight speeds, comes in many different colors, and has more options, which also means it might take some extra time and research to be thoroughly understood. But this means that if it's right for you, it can be even more customizable and fine-tuned to your specific needs.

The major differences:
- Flexible premium
- Increasing policy costs
- Transparency

Let's start with those increasing policy costs. Basically, the underlying cost of insurance based on your probability of dying increases as you age. This is similar to a term insurance policy except that with universal life, the computer typically solves for a level premium you can pay to maintain that coverage through life expectancy as opposed to a designated period of time with term coverage.

A universal life policy also provides transparency in showing you its various expenses, such as mortality costs, administration costs, and interest credited. It becomes easier for the consumer to see exactly what they are being charged each year, which makes it different from a whole life policy that provides only a summary of your cash value and the amount of any dividend that has been paid or reinvested. With a whole life policy, it's almost impossible, in our opinion, to accurately know how the insurance company determines the costs you are charged or the dividends you might receive.

Remember how whole life policies have those actuaries at the insurer's office calculating all of that and then determining a set rate for you to pay to cover it all? Well, with universal life, that's part of the flexible premium part. You can decide to pay a premium that will cover your future policy expenses, or you can pay a premium that barely covers your current policy expenses, depending on your circumstances.

That is where these policies have gotten a bad rap in the past. If you purchase a policy and only pay the minimum premium required, your policy would never build up any cash value to offset the increased cost of insurance when you are older and more likely to die. Thus, the cost would increase each year and your policy will likely get too expensive to continue later on.

Having said that, if your goal is inexpensive insurance coverage for life, you could set up a universal life policy to run like a term insurance policy with a conservative interest rate and level funding. This would cost much less than whole life because it would not build any real cash value. Now, you might have to make a few tweaks in later years if your premiums are not meeting the increased costs of insurance as you get older. You also have the option of funding a universal life policy as you would a whole life policy with higher annual premiums but also with the flexibility to lower those premiums for a year or two, or even skip them for a short term, if the need arises.

We suggest the complexity and variety of these products are why it's incredibly important to work with a financial advisor you trust. This should be someone who is independent and who gives you the straight story about which kind of product would be appropriate for you and who makes sure you fully understand all the details.

To return to our example of Emma, here's how a well-set-up universal life insurance policy could work: Emma, ever the diligent saver, would have paid well over the minimum premium every month. Every time she got a raise or payroll increase, she increased the amount of premium she paid into her policy. With the policy's contractual rate of interest, she had a substantial amount of cash value accumulated in the policy. That way, when she decided to borrow money against the policy to help her brother, she could even afford to decrease her monthly payments for a time until she was back in a better financial position.

Variable and Indexed Life

Now to the main event: variable and indexed universal life insurance, or VUL and IUL. Like any permanent insurance, a VUL or IUL policy will remain in force as long as you continue to pay sufficient premiums, and you can borrow against your policy's cash value, income-tax-free. In addition, VUL and IUL policies are, at their core, universal life insurance policies with that flexible premium. So, how are they different?

If you skim back through some of the other policy details, we covered the ability to withdraw or borrow some of the cash value of your policy without paying income taxes. These two types of universal life policies differ from what we previously discussed as they both outsource some of the investment decisions to you, the policyholder.

With VUL, you get to choose how to invest the excess premiums being paid during the early years into mutual fund sub-accounts that look a lot like your investment choices in a 401(k) plan. If you are young and have more years to weather ups and downs in the market, you could ultimately earn more on your cash value than from the performance of the general assets of the insurance company. But if you are buying the insurance for the guarantees, this might not be the best option for you.

With an IUL policy, your cash accumulation can be credited interest based on whatever your policy's index is. An index is a tool that measures the movement of the market, like the S&P

500, or the Dow Jones Industrial Average. (You can't invest directly in an index; it's just a sort of ruler.)

The amount of interest credited to your policy is limited by a "cap" or other limits such as a spread or participation rate. But an IUL also offers a downside limit, commonly called a "floor." The "indexed" option allows your cash value to earn potentially greater returns than a standard universal life policy in a year when the market goes up, but also sets a floor of either zero or 1 percent if the market goes down and the index shows negative returns.

So, for example, let's say your contract cap is 12.5 percent and the floor is 0 percent. If the market returns 20 percent, your contract value gets a 12.5 percent interest credit. The next year, the S&P 500 returns a negative 26 percent. The insurance company won't credit your policy anything, but you also won't see your policy value slip because of that negative performance (although policy charges and expenses will still be deducted from your policy). So, your policy won't lose value because of poor market conditions, but you can still stand to realize interest credits due to changes in an index.

So, back to our friend, Emma. If her permanent life insurance policy was an IUL, what might that have looked like? Emma saves, paying well over the mandatory minimum of her IUL policy. Let's assume the market does well for decades. Her policy accumulates a significant cash value. At some point, she stops paying as much in premium, or maybe she stops paying any premium at all from her own pocket because her policy has enough in cash value that it is paying for its own expenses with the insurance company. Then, when her brother needs help, there is enough cash value stored in the policy that she can take out a tax-free loan to help her sibling.

It's important to note that making withdrawals or taking policy loans from a policy may have an adverse effect. You may want to talk to your financial advisor to re-evaluate your premium payment schedule if you are considering this option.

A Tax-Advantaged Investment Vehicle

The tax rules around life insurance make it a great alternative to more standard investments inside of a tax-advantaged wrapper. The cash value growth or earnings of life insurance are not taxed unless you surrender a policy or withdraw more than you pay in. In addition, borrowing from a policy is also not a taxable event as long as the policy is structured properly and stays in force. And the death benefit is also income tax free, and if owned outside of your estate, it can be estate-tax free. Therefore, life insurance has tax properties that make it look and feel like a Roth IRA without all the restrictions.

When using life insurance as a savings/investment vehicle you would typically overfund the policy, paying in as much as you want to invest and buying as little death benefit as possible so that it is still considered life insurance. You would pick the type of policy based on your goals and risk tolerance. If you wanted to be able to direct investments into mutual funds or target-date funds, then variable life is likely your product. If you want upside potential while limiting losses if the markets decline, then indexed life might be a better fit. If you want bond-like returns, then you might look to whole life.

If you're now reeling just a bit, it's understandable. There's a lot going on with these policies. But if you don't take the time to understand the basics of how they work, it's entirely possible to fall behind on premium payments and end up with a policy that lapses. If, however, you understand the terms of your contract and are working with purpose, a VUL or an IUL could be a powerful cog in the greater mechanics of your overall investment strategy.

CHAPTER 10

Long-Term Care Insurance

E arlier in this book, we've outlined the risks longevity poses to your financial health. In fact, you may be tired of hearing it at this point.

Even so, we'd still like to repeat one more time—in case you've forgotten—it's estimated *seven* out of every ten Americans who reach age sixty-five will need long-term care of some kind.[65] And so we ask: If you knew the car you were going to be riding in had a 70 percent chance of having an accident, would you wear your seatbelt?

From Aviva Sapers: All three of my grandparents, as well as my in-laws and my mother, have all needed round-the-clock care at some point in their lives. My in-laws, for many years, needed multiple caregivers.

After my grandmother had her stroke, she was tube fed for more than four years. Even though my grandfather was alive, he was unable to take care of her by himself given that he was in his eighties and she was unable to move herself from a bed to a chair or anywhere else. During that time, my grandfather and father paid over $1 million out of pocket for caregiver assistance. Luckily, they could afford it, but it was a significant cost nonetheless.

One of my clients to whom we sold long-term care insurance (LTCI) asked me after her husband had a stroke

111

whether she could afford to have him receive care at home for his final years. I said, "Of course, that is what the long-term care insurance is for." At his funeral, she kept telling people that it was because of me and the LTCI I sold her that her husband was able to live his last three years at home. Years later she developed dementia and used her LTCI to cover the costs of her caregivers.

The bottom line is we need to do a better job of planning for the possibility of a long-term illness.

Earlier in the book, we covered the various ways of paying for our own possible long-term care costs, from self-funding to insurance riders. We'd like to take a moment to expand on what is one of the most comprehensive coverage options: long-term care insurance.

LTCI Basics

The long-term care insurance space has had a bit of a shakeup in the past few years. Many insurers stopped offering LTCI, and the stand-alone policies remaining are often more expensive. In addition, denials of LTCI applications have risen to the point that 38.2 percent of those between the ages of sixty-five and sixty-nine are rejected. The percentage increases to 47 percent for applicants aged seventy to seventy-five.[66]

Yet, the other side of the coin is the insurers who are left in the stand-alone LTCI space have experience and policies that have endured. LTCI may be more expensive for individuals, but that's because the costs can be more expensive for insurers and because overall long-term care is just plain expensive, period. It's important to understand LTCI carriers aren't making money hand-over-fist with these products. Instead, the carriers who have stopped selling policies were likely carriers who had unrealistic prices and underperforming policies. Prices have stabilized, according to one report, yet could still be considered expensive to some.[67]

While many criticize the use-it-or-lose-it nature of LTCI, it is reasonable to consider that homeowner's insurance, car insurance, term life insurance, and many other types of insurance work the same way. Yes, you are paying into a policy in the hopes you may never use it. But, if you must use it, it can provide value well beyond the actual dollars you have paid into it. An average of 358,500 experience a structural home fire every year[68] for the 131.2 million households in the United States,[69] you have *less than a half a percent chance* of experiencing a home fire in any given year. Yet most of us would still squirm at the thought of not having homeowner's or renter's insurance to cover fire damage. Paradoxically, while LongTermCare.gov says that those among us turning sixty-five stand a 70 percent chance of needing long-term care, only 10 percent of Americans have LTCI.[70]

To purchase LTCI, you have to complete an application that includes a medical questionnaire. Depending on your age and the insurance carrier, you may also need to complete a medical exam. If you qualify, then the insurance company will offer you a policy with certain coverage and pricing based on the probability of needing long-term care in the future. The younger you are, the more likely you are to qualify for insurance—at a rate that is more likely affordable for you.

LTCI premiums count as medical expenses and may potentially be paid with special tax considerations. For instance, if you are eligible to itemize your medical expenses, LTCI premiums can be itemized. Or, alternately, you can pay premiums with tax-free money in health savings accounts. The amount you can withdraw tax-free for LTCI premiums depends on your age.

If you have an LTCI policy, coverage will typically kick in when you have been medically shown to be unable to perform two or more activities of daily living (ADLs). An ADL is an activity such as bathing, toileting, eating, dressing, transferring, and continence; or if you are cognitively impaired. These are all things we naturally prefer to do by ourselves; they are markers of our independence and ability to take care of ourselves. But once someone is unable to do some of these things alone, they will likely need long-term help.

So, if you have LTCI, once you reach this point you will qualify for a daily amount of coverage over a pre-selected time period, depending on the terms of your policy. That money could be used to cover the cost of a nursing home, in-home care, or community organization care. The benefits will begin after the policy's elimination period, which you choose when you purchase the policy. The elimination period can range from 0 to 180 days. The shorter the elimination period, the higher the premium.

With LTCI, you can pick and choose facilities or care options according to your standards instead of having the government decide what is best for you.

Other LTC Products

Life insurance with a long-term care rider was many insurance companies' answer to withdrawing from the LTC market. With a permanent life policy, you can purchase an LTC rider which allows early access to the policy's death benefit should you need it for long-term care. It is typically 2 to 4 percent of the death benefit paid out monthly until the death benefit is depleted. The monthly benefit does not change over time, so if you use the benefit in the early years of needing care, it will likely be more than you need. If used in the later years, it could be less than you require. You still need to qualify by not being able to perform two of six activities of daily living or being cognitively impaired. However, if you never use the benefit, your beneficiaries receive the full death benefit when you pass.

The other "use it or keep it option" is a hybrid policy—a life insurance policy with a death benefit not much larger than the premiums paid, but often provides a pool of money to cover LTC needs. The pool typically equals about three to five times what is paid in, and it looks like a stand-alone LTC policy in many ways. The major difference is, if you don't use the LTC coverage, your family receives a death benefit equal to at least what was paid in premiums. It has the typical features of a monthly benefit, optional inflation riders, an elimination period, and a set pool of money from which to draw.

Both these options are typically used for limited-pay scenarios. However, unlike the stand-alone LTCI products, the premiums on these life insurance policies with LTC riders can be guaranteed whereas the premiums on stand-alone policies are not.

Long-Term Care Partnership Program

One other significant advantage of LTCI is many plans are eligible for a federal-state government initiative called the Long-Term Care Partnership Program.[71] This program is a joint effort by the federal government and certain states to help individuals decide to choose LTCI protection. (Our home state of Massachusetts does not currently offer one of these programs.) The program provides that if you deplete your LTCI coverage and find yourself in a position of having to spend down your assets to become eligible for Medicaid, part or all of your LTCI coverage limit will extend to your assets. Here's what this might look like "in real life" (using, of course, a completely hypothetical person):

Jennifer chooses an LTCI policy to cover up to three years of nursing home care (a little more than the average long-term care stay) in a semi-private room. After several injuries render her unable to dress or bathe herself, Jennifer moves to a retirement community. Jennifer is not average. Her policy has paid out more than $250,000 on her behalf, and her policy benefits are now exhausted. This puts her in position for a Medicaid spend down. However, because she purchased a policy her state approved in line with the Long-Term Care Partnership Program, instead of having to spend down her assets to the Medicaid requirement and leaving very little for her family to inherit, she is allowed to set aside $250,000 on top of her state's other spend-down exemptions.[72]

LTCI — It's Not Just About You

Aside from the aforementioned partnership program and possible tax advantages of traditional LTCI, we think perhaps one of the most compelling arguments in favor of preparing for the likelihood of long-term care has less to do with our own personal assets and more to do with others.

What do we mean? Well, we often hear people tell us, "I don't want to become a financial burden to my kids."

Like estate planning, long-term care planning isn't solely about us. In fact, we might argue that the most important piece of long-term care planning isn't about you at all. It's about your loved ones. It's about your spouse, your children, or your friends, and how caring for you could impact them if you don't have the necessary resources.

Most caregiving for the elderly happens in people's private homes. A survey of caregivers reveals just a sampling of how a long stint of caring for relatives and loved ones can affect the caregivers:[73]

- Of those surveyed, a mean of nineteen hours a week was provided in care. Among those, about 38 percent had to cut back their hours at their job
- More than half reported that their personal and mental health was impacted, including depression and a lower standard of living

- 66 percent of caregivers used their personal assets, like savings and retirement funds, to pay for a loved one's care
- 52 percent of caregivers moved closer to the loved one for whom they provided care

We believe LTCI is an important part of everyone's financial plan. No one wants to pay for caregivers or nursing homes out of pocket. And for many, the cost of these services can completely destroy one's lifetime savings–especially retirement savings. LTCI, in our opinion, is the most cost-effective way to pay for costs we are quite likely to incur at some point in our lives.

Of course, some people believe they are wealthy enough to self-insure. But even they might appreciate that a stand-alone LTCI policy whose benefits you utilize can provide between a 10 to 14 percent rate of return on one's money.

If you aren't willing to take the risk of a use-it-or-lose-it strategy, then a hybrid product or life insurance with an LTC rider would be good options. This way, if you never get sick and need the LTC coverage—and we hope that you don't—your family can recover the cost of the additional coverage through the tax-free death benefit they will receive when you pass on.

Because of its benefits for both the policyholder and his or her family or caregiver, LTCI can be a valuable asset in any retirement plan.

CHAPTER 11

Estate & Legacy

I n our practice, we devote a significant portion of our time to matters of estates. That doesn't mean drawing up wills or trusts or putting together powers of attorney or anything like that. After all, we're not estate planning attorneys. But we are financial advisors, and what part of the "estate" isn't affected by money matters?

We've included this chapter because we have seen many people do estate planning wrong. Clients, or clients' families, have come in after experiencing a death in the family and have found themselves in the middle of probate, high taxes, or a discovery of something unforeseen (like long-term care expenses) draining the estate.

We have also seen people do estate planning right: families who visit our office to talk about legacies and how to make them last and adult children who have room to grieve without an added burden of unintended costs, without stress from a family ruptured because of inadequate planning.

We'll share some of these stories here. However, we're not going to give you specific advice, since everyone's situation is unique. But we do want to give you some things to think about and underscore the importance of planning ahead.

Consider a situation we encountered in which a widower father thought he was doing everything right in preparing a will that instructed his three sons to sell his home—a million-dollar property—and split the proceeds three ways. Simple, right?

Hardly. Because Dad left no other liquid assets, his sons were left to pay out of pocket for the funeral expenses, the real estate taxes, and other estate-settling matters. One sibling who was not in a good financial place spent the days leading up to the funeral, and immediately afterward, lobbying his brothers for a quick sale of Dad's house so that he could get his share of the inheritance. His brothers, who had to foot his share of the funeral expenses and taxes, weren't in a hurry to get baby brother his money, and it created a family squabble that, to our understanding, is ongoing. The last we heard, two of the brothers still weren't talking to the third. This scenario is all too common.

We know of other situations where parents wanted to leave a vacation home on Cape Cod to their kids—ostensibly to provide a place for family members to gather and vacation as a family. Nice idea.

But then you have one adult child who doesn't live in the area and doesn't get to use the family home as much as their siblings. They become resentful when asked to pay their share of taxes and upkeep on the house. They will likely push to sell the house in the belief that money in their hand now is worth more than a walk on the beach on some future summer day. Or, one of the kids might use the home on a more regular basis than the others, and that can lead to arguments over the fair share of upkeep. And if the regular user wants the home but can't buy out the shares of the others, you have the seeds for even more discontent. This doesn't even include the time and effort needed to pay the bills, clean the home, make repairs etc.

Over time, the parents' dream of having a family gathering place might do more to drive the children further apart.

Throughout this chapter, we'll convey legal means to avoid messy estate issues, especially the perils of probate. There are ways to make the passing of your assets to future generations go as smoothly as possible, and we encourage you to consider the use of the estate-planning tools we'll explain here.

Sadly, we've also come to accept that even the best plan is fraught with challenges, and sometimes good intentions cannot overcome a bad family dynamic. But by planning in advance, you can at least try to minimize the chaos.

You Can't Take It With You

When it comes to legacy and estate planning, the most important thing is to do it. We have heard people from clients to celebrities (rap artist Snoop Dogg comes to mind) say they aren't interested in what happens to their assets when they die because they'll be dead. That's certainly one way to look at it.

But we think the majority of people think differently—we all have people and causes we care about, and those who care about us. Even if the people we love don't *need* what we leave behind, these assets can still be legally tied up in the probate process or burial costs if we don't plan. And that's not even considering what happens if you become incapacitated at some point while you are still alive. Having a plan in place can greatly reduce the stress of those responsibilities on your loved ones.

Estate Documents

There are a few documents that lay the groundwork of legacy planning. You've probably heard of some (if not all) of them, but we'd like to review what they are and how people commonly use them. These are all things you should talk about with an estate planning attorney to establish your legacy.

Powers of Attorney

A power of attorney, or POA, is a document giving someone the authority to act on your behalf and in your best interests. These come in handy in situations where you cannot be present (imagine a vacation where you get stuck overseas) or, when you are incapacitated (as in a coma or coping with dementia).

It is important to have powers of attorney in place and to appoint someone you trust to act on your behalf in these matters. Have you ever heard of someone who was incapacitated after a car accident, whether from head trauma or being in a coma for weeks—sometimes months? Do you think their bills stopped coming due during that time? Who is paying the phone bill? Utility bills? Real estate taxes? A power of attorney would grant the authority to pay your mortgage or cancel your cable while you are unable to.

You can have multiple POAs and require them to act jointly.

Do you think two heads are better than one? One man, Chris, significantly relied on his two sons' opinions for both his business and personal matters. He appointed both sons as joint POA, requiring both their signoffs for his medical and financial matters.

You can have multiple POAs who can act independently.

What this looks like: Irene had three children with whom she routinely stayed. They lived in different areas of the country, which she thought was an advantage; one month she might be hiking out West, the next she could enjoy the newest off-Broadway production, and the next she could soak up some Southern sun. She named her three children as independently authorized POAs so that if something happened, no matter where she was, the child closest could step in to act on her behalf.

You can have POAs who have different responsibilities.
What this looks like: Although Luke's friend Claire, a nurse, was his go-to and POA for health-related issues, financial matters usually made her nervous, so he appointed his good neighbor, Matt, as his POA in all of his financial and legal matters.

In addition to POAs, it may be helpful to have an advanced medical directive. This is a document where you have pre-decided what choices you would make about different health scenarios. An advanced medical directive can help ease the burden for your medical POA and loved ones, particularly when it comes to end-of-life care.

There are many famous musicians who have died without a will, and unfortunately (if they were successful), their estates keep receiving money in royalties which complicates things even further. Take Jimi Hendrix or Bob Marley. They both died without wills and battles over their estates raged on for years afterwards. When Pablo Picasso died at the age of ninety-one, he left behind a fortune in assets that included artwork, five homes, cash, gold, and bonds. Because Picasso died intestate—without a will—it took six years to settle his estate at a cost of $30 million. His assets were eventually divided among six heirs.

Wills

Perhaps the most basic document of legacy planning, a will, is a legal document wherein you outline your wishes for your estate. When it comes to your estate after your death, having a will is the foundation of your legacy. Without one, your loved ones are left guessing what you would have wanted, and the probate court will likely split your assets according to the state's defaults. Maybe that's exactly what you wanted. Or maybe it isn't. Because even if you told your nephew he could have your car he's been driving, if it's not in writing, it still might go to the brother, sister, son, or daughter to whom you aren't speaking.

However, it may not be enough just to have a will. Even with a will, your assets will still be subject to probate. Probate is what we call the state's process for determining a will's validity. A judge will go through your will to question if it conflicts with state law, if it is the most up-to-date document, if you were mentally competent at the time it was in order, etc. For some, this is a quick, easily-resolved process. For others, particularly if someone steps forward to contest the will, it may take years to settle, all the while subjecting the assets to court costs and attorney's fees.

One other undesirable piece of the probate process is that it is a public procedure. That means anyone can go to the courthouse, ask for copies of the case, and discover your assets. They can also see who is slated to receive what and who is disputing.

Even having a will can sometimes result in difficulty. Especially if there are multiple changes to a will, or—and this can happen—evidence of multiple wills.

Aretha Franklin's estate, for example, became a major headache for her loved ones. Her lawyer presented her will with four documents, handwritten and barely legible. The possibility of tampering or forgery made the documents questionable as evidence in court. Aretha passed on Aug. 16, 2018, and as this book was being completed in 2023, her estate was still unsettled.

Although her alleged wills show that Aretha was clearly concerned for the well-being of her loved ones and wanted them to share her fortune, the late singer's haphazard planning pitted brother against brother, exposed dark family secrets, and jeopardized millions of dollars intended for family members but might instead go to the IRS. Perhaps worst of all, the legendary singer was notoriously private, and now all of this is being played out in news headlines for the entire world to see.

Talk about showing the Queen of Soul no R-E-S-P-E-C-T!

It's also important to remember beneficiary lines trump wills. So, that large life insurance policy? What if, when you bought it fifteen years ago, you wrote your ex-husband's name on the beneficiary line? Even if you stipulate otherwise in your will, the company that holds your policy will pay out to your ex-spouse. Or, how about the thousands of dollars in your IRA you dedicated to your children thirty years ago, but one of them passed unexpectantly, leaving his wife and two toddlers behind? That IRA may transfer to your remaining children, with nothing for your daughter-in-law and grandchildren.

That may paint a grim portrait, but we can't underscore enough the importance of working with a skilled estate planning attorney to keep your will and beneficiary lines up to date as your life changes.

Again, as noted previously, we are not estate attorneys, but we work closely with many people who are. This close working relationship allows us to make sure the estate attorneys we deal with understand the concepts we tend to recommend. They understand the role insurance plays in our planning process and what it can mean in estate planning. When working together, we often provide them with client notes and summaries of assets and goals, as well as personal balance sheets. The lawyers we work with tell us that receiving this ongoing communication about clients helps them more quickly identify areas they might want to address with our client at a later time.

Trusts

Another piece of legacy planning to consider is a trust.

A trust allows a third party, or trustee, to hold your assets and determine how they will pass to your beneficiaries. Many people are skeptical of trusts because they assume trusts are only appropriate for the fabulously wealthy, but they are employed routinely to aid in the orderly transfer of assets for people of all income levels. A trust can help you avoid both the expense and public exposure of probate, provide a more immediate transfer of wealth, avoid some taxes, and provide you greater control over your legacy.

For instance, if you want to set aside some funds for a grandchild's college education, you can make it a requirement that he or she enrolls in classes before your trust will dispense any funds. Or, you can establish a trust to provide for the medical, educational or basic lifestyle needs of an adult child, but also stipulate that their children not receive any trust disbursements until they turn thirty years old. Note, too, that like a will, beneficiary lines will override your trust conditions, so you must still keep insurance policies and other assets up to date.

Like any financial or legal consideration, there are many options these days beyond the simple "yes or no" question of whether to have a trust. For one thing, you will need to consider if you want your trust to be revocable (you can change the terms while you are alive) or irrevocable (can't be changed; you are no longer the "owner" of the contents).

A brief note here about irrevocable trusts: Although they have significant tax benefits, they are still subject to a Medicaid look-back period. This means, if you transfer your assets into an irrevocable trust in an attempt to shelter them from a Medicaid spend-down, you will be ineligible for Medicaid coverage of long-term care for five years. Yet, an irrevocable trust can avoid both probate and estate taxes, and it can even protect assets from legal judgments against you.

Another thing to remember when it comes to trusts is that it is not enough to just establish one; you also must fund it. We've had numerous clients come to us assuming they have protected their assets with a trust. When we talk about taxes and other pieces of their legacy, it turns out they never retitled any assets or changed any paperwork on the assets they wanted in the trust. So, please remember, a trust is just a bunch of fancy legal papers if you haven't followed through on retitling your assets.

Taxes

Although charitable contributions, trusts, and other tax-efficient strategies can reduce your tax bill, it's unlikely your estate will be passed on entirely tax-free. Yet, when it comes to building a legacy that can last for generations, taxes can be one of the heaviest drains on the impact of your hard work.

For 2023, the federal estate exemption was $12.92 million per individual and $25.84 million for a married couple, with estates facing up to a 40 percent tax rate after that. Currently, the new estate limits are set to increase with inflation until January 1, 2026, when they will "sunset" back to the inflation-adjusted 2017 limits.[74] And that's not taking into account the various state regulations and taxes regarding estate and inheritance transfers.

Another "frequent flyer" among tax concerns: retirement accounts.

Your IRA or 401(k) can be a source of tax issues when you pass away. For one thing, taking funds from a sizable retirement account can trigger a large tax bill. However, if you leave the assets in the account, there are still required minimum distributions (RMDs), which will take effect even after you die. If you pass the account to your spouse, he or she can keep taking your RMDs as is, or your spouse can retitle the account in his or her name and receive RMDs based on his or her life expectancy.

Remember, if you don't take your RMDs, the IRS will impose a penalty of up to 25 percent of your required distribution, You will still have to pay income taxes whenever you withdraw that money. Provisions in the original SECURE Act of 2019 require that anyone who inherits your IRA, with few exceptions (your spouse, a beneficiary less than ten years younger, or a disabled adult child, to name a few), will need to empty the account within ten years of your death.

Also—and this is a pretty big also—check with an attorney if you are considering putting your IRA or 401(k) in a trust. An improperly titled beneficiary form for the IRA could mean the difference of thousands of dollars in taxes. This is just one more reason to work with a financial advisor, one who can strategically partner with an estate planning attorney to diligently check your decisions.

CHAPTER 12

Women Retire Too

W e help men, women, and families from all walks of life on their journey to and through retirement. Yet, we want to address the female demographic specifically. Why? To be perfectly blunt, women—in our opinion—tend to do more research and want more education before making financial decisions. The topics, products, and strategies we cover elsewhere in this book are meant to help address retirement concerns for men *and* women. However, women's career paths often look much different than men's, so why would their retirement planning look the same?

Women often embrace different roles and values than men as workers, wives, mothers, and daughters. They are more apt to take on roles as caretakers. They often tend to be planners for life events, worry about loved ones, tend to details, and think about the future.

If these characteristics of women are accurate, shouldn't they deserve special considerations from financial advisors? The case can be made, particularly since 69 percent of men in the U.S. age 65 and older happen to be married compared to 47 percent of women in that age classification.[75] Single women don't have the opportunity to capitalize on the resource pooling and potential economies of scale accompanying a marriage or partnership.

For a long time, many women gave up their careers and stayed home to raise their kids. That changed over time as many households needed two wage earners to support themselves. But as much as progress has advanced in the number of women-owned businesses and pay parity between men and women, statistics still show that women are the main caregivers of their kids and their parents. This often limits their ability to be the main breadwinners.

Given that women statistically live longer than men and might be less willing to take risk, we take all these factors into account when working with them on a financial plan. They certainly need an equal voice at the table.

Be Informed

It's a familiar scene in many financial offices across the country: A woman of our mother's generation comes into an appointment carrying a sack full of unopened envelopes. She sits across the desk from a financial advisor and apologizes her way through a conversation about what financial products she owns and where her income is coming from. She is recently widowed and was sure her spouse was taking care of the finances, but now she doesn't know where all their assets are kept, and her confidence in her financial outlook has wavered after walking through funeral expenses and realizing she's down to one income.

Often, she may be financially "okay." Yet, the uncertainty can be wearying, particularly when the family is already reeling from a loss. While this scenario sometimes plays out with men, in our experience, it's more likely to be a woman in that chair across from our conference table, probably, in part, because of Western traditions about money management being "a guy thing." But it doesn't have to be this way. This all-too-common scenario can be wiped away with just a little preparation.

From Aviva Sapers: As most women outlive men, it is not uncommon for older women to eventually have to fend for themselves whether or not they are set up to do so. I remember when my eighty-six-year-old grandmother passed and I ended up driving many of her friends to the gravesite. I expected on the trip over to hear all sorts of memories and accolades about my grandmother, Ann. Instead, and to my surprise, Ann's friends, widows all, spent much of their time talking about how they'd had to become financially astute when living on their own. They talked about how much they were earning in their money market accounts and CDs. Clearly, these women, who each had to become self-sufficient, were eager to share their financial learnings in order to help one another.

It would have been much easier if they had been involved in these discussions with their husbands years earlier. Instead, they had to learn about their financial lives under fire at much older ages. With more advanced planning and preparation, they also might have been less worried about how they would continue to produce the cash flow necessary to pay the bills and meet their basic needs.

In our generation, this is a less likely occurrence. Many women have reached out to learn more about finances and investments, and we arc happy to help them. Many women have joined investment clubs to have a place to learn about investing and to create their own support group to help them learn together. Regardless, we have created a series entitled "Women Getting Wise About Wealth" to help women of any generation learn the language of financial vehicles so they can be better informed and begin to know the questions to ask.

Talk to Your Spouse/
Work with a Financial Advisor

While there are many factors affecting women's financial preparation for and situations in retirement, we cannot emphasize enough that the decision to be informed, to be a part of the conversation and to be aware of what is going on with your finances is absolutely paramount to a confident retirement.

In most couples we see, there is almost always an "alpha" when it comes to finances. It isn't always men; for many of our couple clients, the wife is the alpha who keeps the books and budgets and knows where all of the family's assets are, down to the penny. Yet, statistically, among baby boomers it is usually a man who runs the books. However, members of Generation X and younger have evolved. The ratio of male to female financial alphas is evening out, or so we've come to believe based on our experience speaking with couples.

The breakdown happens when there is a lack of communication, when no one other than the financial alpha knows how much the family has and where. In the end, it doesn't matter who handles the money; it's about all parties being informed of what's going on financially.

There are a lot of ways to open the conversation about money. One woman started a conversation with her husband, the financial alpha, by sitting down and saying, "Teach me how to be a widow." Perhaps that sounds grim, but it was to the point, and it spurred what she said was a very fruitful conversation. Couples sometimes have their first real conversation about money, assets, and their retirement income approach, in our office. The important thing about having these conversations isn't where, it's when . . . and the best "when" is as soon as possible.

After the woman asked her husband "to teach her how to be a widow," they spent a day, just one part of an otherwise dull

132

weekend, going through everything she might need to know. They spent the better part of two decades together after that. When he died and she was widowed, she said the "widowhood" talk had made a huge difference. She knew who to call to talk through their retirement plan and where to call for the insurance policy.

She said the fruit of the weekend exercise they engaged in some twenty years earlier couldn't have been more apparent than when she ultimately accompanied a recently widowed friend of hers to a financial appointment. Her friend was emotional the whole time, afraid she would run out of money any day. The financial advisor ultimately showed the friend that she was financially in good shape, but not before the friend had already spent months worried that each check would exhaust her bank account. That's no way to live after losing a loved one. It was preventable had her deceased spouse and financial advisor included her in a conversation about "widowhood."

Spouse-Specific Options

One area where it might be especially important for spouses to be on the same page is when it comes to financial products or services that have spousal options. A few that come to mind are pensions and Social Security, although life insurance and annuity policies also have the potential to affect both spouses.

With pensions, taking the worker's life-only option is somewhat attractive—after all, the monthly payment is bigger when payments are promised to only one person. However, you and your spouse should discuss your options. When we're talking about assuring payments for both of you, as opposed to just one lifespan, there is an increased likelihood at least one of you will live a long, long time. This means the monthly payout will be less, but it also ensures that, no matter which spouse outlives the other, no one will have to suffer the loss of a needed pension paycheck in his or her later retirement years.

While we covered Social Security options in a different chapter, we think some of the spousal information bears repeating. Particularly, if you worked exclusively inside the home for a significant number of years, you may want to talk about taking your Social Security benefits based on your spouse's work history. After all, Social Security is based on your thirty-five highest-earning years.

Things to remember about the spousal benefits:[76]

- Your benefit will be calculated as a percentage (up to 50 percent) of your spouse's earned monthly benefit at his or her full retirement age, or FRA.
- For you to begin receiving a spousal benefit, your spouse must have already filed for his or her own benefits and you must be at least sixty-two.
- You can qualify for a full half of your spouse's benefits if you wait until you reach FRA to file.
- Beginning your benefits earlier than your FRA will reduce your monthly check but waiting to file until after FRA will not increase your benefits.

For divorcees:[77]

- You may qualify for an ex-spousal benefit if . . .
    a. You were married for a decade or more
    b. *and* you are at least sixty-two
    c. *and* you have been divorced for at least two years
    d. *and* you are currently unmarried
    e. *and* your ex-spouse is sixty-two (qualifies to begin taking Social Security)
- Your ex-spouse does not need to have filed for you to file on his or her benefit.

- Similar to spousal benefits, you can qualify for up to half of your ex-spouse's benefits if you wait to file until your FRA.
- If your ex-spouse dies, you may file to receive a widow/widower benefit on his or her Social Security record as long as you are at least age sixty and fulfill all the other requirements on the preceding list.
  a. This will not affect the benefits of your ex-spouse's current spouse

For widows or widowers benefits:[78]
- You may qualify to receive as much as your deceased spouse would have received if . . .
  a. You were married for at least nine months before his or her death
  b. *or* you would qualify for a divorced spousal benefit
  c. *and* you are at least sixty
  d. *and* you did not/have not remarried before age sixty
- You may earn delayed credits on your spouse's benefit *if* your spouse hadn't already filed for benefits when he or she died.
- Other rules may apply to you if you are disabled or are caring for a deceased spouse's dependent or disabled child.

Longevity

On average, women live longer than men. Most stats put average female longevity at about two years more than men. But averages are tricky things. An April 2022 report by the World Economic Forum listed the eight oldest people in the world to all be women. They ranged in age from 114 years old to 118 and included two Americans.[79]

Women may be fabulous and live longer, but living longer presents longstanding financial ramifications.

Because women live longer, they are more likely to become disabled for a longer period of time. The insurance companies are well aware of this statistically because both disability insurance and long-term care insurance cost more for women. At the same time, life insurance is cheaper as it is based on the probability of dying, and women tend to live longer.

Simply Needing More Money in Retirement

Living longer in retirement means needing more money, period. Barring a huge lottery win or some crazy stock market action, the date you retire is likely the point at which you have the most money you will ever have. Not to put too grim a spin on it, but the problem with longevity is, the further you get away from that date, the further your dollars have to stretch. If you planned to live to a nice eighty-something but live to a nice one-hundred-something, that is two decades you will need to account for, monetarily.

To put this in perspective, let's say you like to drink coffee as an everyday splurge. Not accounting for inflation, a $2.50 cup-a-day habit is $18,250 over a two-decade span. Now, think of all the things you like to do that cost money. Add those up for twenty years of unanticipated costs. We think you'll see what we mean.

During the 2020 onset of the coronavirus pandemic, many learned to cut costs. For some, that amounted to skipping their decadent latte. For others, however, cutbacks became acute. According to data compiled by Age Wave and Edward Jones, 32 percent of Americans plan to retire later than planned because of the pandemic. Women felt a more adverse effect. The report stipulated that 41 percent of women continued to save for retirement, compared to 58 percent of men.[80]

More Health Care Needs

Adding to the cost of living a longer life is the fact that aging, plain and simple, means more health care, and more health care requires more money. Women are survivors. They suffer from the morbidity-mortality paradox, which states women suffer more non-fatal illnesses throughout their lifetime than men, who experience fewer illnesses but higher mortality.

Women have been found to seek treatment more often when not feeling well and emphasize staying healthy when older, according to studies. Survival, we believe, is on the side of the woman. However, surviving things, like cancer, also means more checkups later in life.

A statistical concern for women involves the prospect of long-term care. Long-term care for women lasts 3.7 years on average compared to 2.2 years for men.[81]

Widowhood

Not only do women typically live longer than their same-age male counterparts, they also stand a greater chance of living alone as they age. Some divorce, separate or never marry. Among those age sixty-five and over, 33 percent of women live alone compared to 20 percent of men.[82]

We don't write this to scare people; rather, we think it's fundamentally important to prepare our female clients for something that may be a startling, *but very likely,* scenario. At some point, most women will have to handle their financial situations on their own. A little preparation can go a long way, and having a basic understanding of your household finances and the "who, what, where, and how much" of your family's assets is incredibly useful—it can prevent a tragic situation from being more traumatic.

In our opinion, the financial services industry sometimes underserves women in these situations. Some financial advisors tend to alienate women, even when their spouses are alive. We've heard several stories of women who sat through meeting after meeting without their financial advisor ever addressing a single question to them.

In our firm, when we work with couples, we work hard to make sure our retirement income strategies work for *both* people. No matter who the financial alpha is, it's important for everyone affected by a retirement strategy to understand it.

In our education series entitled "Women Getting Wise About Wealth" (WGWAW), we believe we've developed a program that helps women become familiar with the terminology and basic concepts of investing and estate planning. We provide as much information as they would like, but will also act as their trusted advisor and create a plan with them to address their cash flow needs and goals, as well as handle their investments and legacy planning.

Taxes

One of the often-unexpected aspects of widowhood is the tax bill. Many women continue similar lifestyles to the ones they shared with their spouses. This, in turn, means continuing to have a similar need for income. However, after the death of a spouse, their taxes will be calculated based on a single filer's income table, which is much less forgiving than the couple's tax rates. With proper planning, your financial advisor and tax advisor may be able to help you take the sting out of your new tax status.

Caregiving

Caregiving.org updates its national report about every five years. According to its findings released in 2020, of the 53 million caregivers providing unpaid, informal care for older adults, 61 percent are women. Among today's family caregivers, 61 percent work and 45 percent report some kind of financial impact from providing a loved one care and support.[83]

In addition to the financial burden created by caregiving responsibilities, women often devote many hours each day to duties such as housekeeping and looking after loved ones. So then, when can women find the time to focus long and hard on financial matters?

Unfortunately, the impact and hardships created by traditional roles for women typically do not account for Social Security benefit losses or the losses of health care benefits and retirement savings. This also doesn't account for maternity care, mothers who homeschool, or women who leave the workforce to care for their children in any way.

We don't repeat these statistics to scare you. Not only are unpaid family caregivers spending their time and energy taking care of others, but they're also putting their own money towards the cause. An AARP study found that three-quarters of family caregivers surveyed were spending an average of $7,242 a year on out-of-pocket caregiving costs.[84] Beyond that, we believe the emotional value of the care many women provide their elderly relatives or neighbors cannot be quantified. So, to be clear, this shouldn't be taken as a "why not to provide caregiving" spiel. Instead, it should be seen as a call for "why to *prepare* for caregiving" or "how to lessen the financial and emotional burden of caregiving."

Funding Your Own Retirement

For these reasons, women need to be prepared to fund more of their own retirements. There are several savings options and products, from annuities and investments to insurance and IRAs. You can never start too soon or save too much. In families where one spouse has dropped out of the workforce to care for a relative, consult your advisor on the best ways to save.

Also, if you find yourself in a caregiving role, talk to your employer's human resources department. Some companies have paid leave, special circumstance, or sick leave options you could qualify for, making it easier to cope and helping you stay in the workforce longer.

Saving Money

Women need more money to fund their retirements, period. But this doesn't have to be a significant burden—often, women are better at saving, while usually taking less risk in their portfolios.[85] This gives us reason to believe, as women continue to get more involved in their finances, families will be better-prepared for retirement.

Charity

Wills and testaments, trusts and powers of attorney—these are all pieces of what we often call legacy planning. But we would be remiss if we didn't address a piece of legacy preparation near and dear to our heart: charitable contributions.

Charity is one of those universal concepts that unites us as human beings. Football players who dedicate their resources to building homes for single moms, communities who help neighbors rebuild after catastrophes, groundskeepers who donate millions from under a mattress to their favorite university, or private donors who put impoverished children through school. . .these are the stories that inspire us, that drive us to be better people.

There are many, many ways to pass money to your favorite charity, university, foundation, or public resource. Some include using qualified charitable distributions with the mandatory withdrawals from your IRA, and others lend themselves to establishing trusts or Donor Advised Funds. Whatever your preferred method of charitable distribution, the right financial advisor will partner with a qualified tax advisor and/or estate planning attorney to discover how to help you make your contributions in a way that fits well within your own strategy for taxes—helping to ensure your contributions pass efficiently to your intended beneficiary.

A client of ours provides an example of things we can do to help fulfill philanthropic goals and mitigate taxes.

This gentleman owned a brownstone in the Back Bay area of Boston and had converted the building into four condominium units. But as he and his wife grew older, the renting and managing of the properties was getting to be too much for them. If they were to sell the condo units, they would have had over $1 million in long-term capital gains with a resulting tax that would take a significant bite out of their life savings.

As an alternative, we suggested that they donate a couple of the condos to a charitable gift annuity (CGA) at his alma mater. A CGA offers a donor a one-time tax deduction for the future value of the donation, and then provides income on the earnings to the donors for either a fixed period of time or the rest of their lives. Our client received what he considered the best of two worlds: 1) a charitable deduction in lieu of paying capital gains taxes, and 2) the creation of a legacy at the medical school that helped train him to be the success he was.

Where to Start?

We've all heard it is better to give than to receive, and science backs this up. Multiple studies show those who give to charity or volunteer experience less depression, lower blood pressure, higher self-esteem, and greater happiness.[86]

It's a common perception, however, that retirees are less inclined to be charitable. It seems like reasoned logic—they're living on fixed incomes, and it's difficult to work charitable giving into conservative strategies designed to protect assets. But this counters the facts. In 2021, more baby boomers donated to charities than any other generations.[87]

So, how do we keep up—or even increase—our donations in retirement? Well, as with all the other topics we cover in this book, step one is to build charitable giving into our financial thinking. Advanced planning can help you be sure your donations—at least in the monetary sense—are given in the most tax-efficient and effective way, both for you and for the charity to which you are contributing.

Planned Giving: Lifetime

When we're talking about charitable contributions, it's important to distinguish between lifetime giving and charitable giving that happens through an estate plan.

The American tax system has many provisions to encourage charitable giving. We're sure the reasoning goes something along the lines of, if we the people were naturally able, through our own means, to care for the poor and vulnerable in our own communities, we collectively would need to pay fewer taxes to support federal aid to those same people. It's a wonderful consideration, and one we should all aspire to. But, in practice, it gets more difficult as tax codes change and shift according to political administrations and other public considerations. Ensuring your charitable contributions are tax-efficient is not a one-time move—it requires yearly analysis.

It's important to remember your charitable giving is most effective when the combined amount of your *itemized* deductions is more than your *standard* deduction. Now it isn't only charity that counts toward your itemized deduction; there are also homeowner and business owner credits, adoption credits, etc. But as it pertains to charity, if you haven't contributed a significant amount to charity in a certain tax year, it may not be worth counting on your taxes.

Deductions change year-to-year, of course, but the IRS usually publishes the following year's charts in November. When you're itemizing deductions, you may deduct up to 50 percent of your adjusted gross (pre-tax) income, though in some cases, 20 percent and 30 percent limitations apply.[88]

Another thing to keep in mind if you are considering the tax implications of a charitable donation, you must have a receipt, a canceled check, or some demonstrable way of recording the transaction. Additionally, many charitable activities aren't eligible for tax credits. Raffle tickets, charity event entrance fees, and those sorts of things are not typically counted as charitable deductions on your taxes. A quick rule of thumb is, if you received something in return for your donation, it's not tax-deductible.

Perhaps one of the most crucial things to keep in mind when it comes to the tax implications of charitable giving, however, is "nonprofit" doesn't mean "tax-advantaged." The IRS keeps a long list of organizations that qualify for tax-deducted gifting in the Internal Revenue Code section 501(c)(3). Yet many excellent nonprofits and civic organizations are not 501(c)(3)s. That doesn't mean you shouldn't give to them—truly, charity is *not* about tax deductions when it comes right down to it—it just means you shouldn't plan to include it as part of your tax-efficiency strategies.

Again, we would be remiss to not emphasize that these laws and definitions change year to year, so it is important to work with a team of qualified financial and tax professionals who can help you plan for the future and adjust to the times, in addition to verifying whether the charity you are considering is tax-exempt.

While impermanence seems to be a fixture of our tax system, one important aspect of charity tax law was made permanent for the foreseeable future. In 2015, Congress passed a budget deal signed into law by President Barack Obama. Among the provisions of the "Protecting Americans From Tax Hikes Act of 2015," which included this important measure:

> IRA charitable rollovers — at age seventy-and-one-half, owners of traditional IRAs can make direct gifts of up to $100,000 a year to a qualified charity directly from

the IRA.[89] This is known as a *qualified charitable distribution or QCD.*

What makes this particular charitable strategy attractive is that a person who uses an IRA to contribute to charity in this way can:

1) Be charitable

2) Avoid having their RMDs push them into a higher tax bracket by instead gifting them to those in need

3) Take advantage of the tax-free aspect of a QCD by not paying income tax on this money leaving their IRA

Let's also note, however, that because IRA contributions can be made after an individual reaches age seventy-three, QCDs will be adversely affected if an IRA contribution is made in the same year a QCD is withdrawn.

The QCD is one tool that can give you a tax benefit for your charitable contribution. A Donor Advised Fund (DAF) is another.

DAFs are a tool we often recommend so that a person can donate appreciated assets in large quantities and receive a tax deduction for the full value of the donation in the tax year of the gift. The fund can then make future gifts to charities of choice (and at the direction of the donor, if desired) over many years to come. Some DAFs can also accept shares of closely held business interest which can have great tax advantages in transferring stock to the next generation of a family business. (A concept for our next book?)

We also created something called the "two-fer" for people who are healthy and have decent-sized group life insurance through work. They can name a charity as the beneficiary of their group life benefit and forgo the taxes due on the attributable income cost for that benefit. Then, for less than the cost of the tax on the attributable income, one can purchase term life insurance and name their family the beneficiary of the individual policy. They thus have two beneficiaries for the price of one.

Planned Giving: After My Lifetime

For many charities, endowments and legacy gifts are the lifeblood that keeps them going. And, for many of us, a large final gift is an excellent way to continue a legacy of giving into perpetuity. There are many financial reasons for charitable bequests, much like the annual contributions we often give, and many reasons are tax-based. A large final gift can be a good way to reduce your taxable estate and create a legacy for a cause of which you are passionate. You could also leave assets when you pass to a DAF placing your kids in the driver's seat to allocate distributions to charities of their choice over their lifetimes.

Many charities have gone to great lengths to make this an attractive option, with some having preferences for certain donation types and strategies. For instance, many public entities, such as libraries and schools, have foundations to collect most of the donations and do major fundraising. Churches and universities often have special projects and intentional funding that stems from sizable endowments.

There are many financial vehicles to help you meet your charitable goals and give you benefits during your lifetime as well—from permanent life insurance policies to charitable trusts and charitable annuities. That's why it's important to plan ahead and work with a goal in mind. If you have some idea of what end you want to achieve, it can be easier to find the estate attorneys, tax professionals, and financial advisors who will be best qualified to help.

Non-Monetary Charitable Contributions

Ultimately, aside from the tax breaks, the good feeling, and the name on a park bench you might receive, your charitable contributions aren't about what you "get" in return. This is one other reason we should plan ahead for our good works— it's about doing the right thing.

Volunteering is one great, non-monetary way to support the charities and causes you believe in. As we noted earlier, research shows retirees who are active and engaged volunteers in their communities often have a better sense of purpose and report more happiness than those who aren't. In volunteering, we have a reason to get up in the morning, and we meet new people and make friends. These are all things that may previously have stemmed from your nine-to-five workday but tend to fall by the wayside after leaving the workforce, thus making this consideration even more important.

From Aviva Sapers: My parents raised us to believe that if we were lucky enough to do well, it was important to give back and to help those less fortunate than ourselves. Over the years, Andrew and I along with our staff have taken at least a half-day off from work and volunteered at The Greater Boston Food Bank, Community Servings, or Cradles to Crayons to name a few charitable service organizations. We have also collected coats, socks, and food for those in need. It was great working as a team, knowing that our actions were put to good use to help others.

I have been involved with Combined Jewish Philanthropies since I was in my twenties. At the time, the Jewish Federations of America were like the mutual funds of the Jewish philanthropic world. The leaders of the community would meet to determine the needs and then would allocate from a central fundraising effort to each agency an amount they felt was appropriate. My involvement was a great way to learn about the needs of the Jewish community both in Boston as well as throughout the U.S. and abroad. I also served on different boards and as chair of many different leadership positions in this organization. And while I donated time and money to the cause, I also made lifelong friends with shared interests. I have brought hundreds of people to Israel to help get them excited about their Judaism, and I learned how to be a better leader.

Another organization I have loved being involved in is the Berklee School of Music. I was lucky to be asked to be part of the president's advisory council at the school because my mother was a trustee. Additionally, my grandfather not only headed up the Brass department many years ago, but also helped to name the school. It is an incredible institution that brings kids from all over the world together to study music, performance, and production. As a trumpet player from my youth, I am in awe of the level of talented students who attend the college and who go off to do amazing things in the world of music.

My involvement here not only has allowed me to continue a family legacy, but it has taken us to the Graduate School in Valencia, Italy, and to the Jazz Festival in Umbria. Music is a big passion of mine and a great way to bring people together around a unifying and empowering experience as opposed to all the political angst throughout the world.

Our families are one way we leave a legacy. But charitable giving—with our time, our talents, and our treasure—allows us to extend our legacies even further.

CHAPTER 14

Help Is At Hand

You've now reached the end of our book. Congratulations on taking the next steps—or perhaps the first steps for some—on the road into a new and potentially exciting phase of your life.

We want to thank you for staying with us to this point. We trust that we were able to provide the kind of helpful information and professional insight to help you achieve financial independence in the years approaching and into retirement. We hope we've been able to address many of the questions you have now, as well as some you will undoubtedly encounter in the near future.

Now let's review some of what you've learned over the course of this journey.

Consider the following more like a pop quiz than a final exam; no all-night study session is required here! Still, let's see how well you can answer the following questions based on what you've read in the previous pages. Note that this is a multiple-choice quiz, and—hint—there will be more than one correct answer for each question. Yes, it's that easy, so let's begin.

What do you know now about when to begin taking Social Security benefits?

   a. My full benefit based on my work history becomes available at my full retirement age (FRA).

b. My benefit will be **permanently reduced** if I take it "early," as soon as age sixty-two.
c. My benefit will be **increased** by 8 percent each year I delay taking benefits between FRA and age seventy.
d. Why are you even asking? Social Security will be broke by the time I'm ready.

How much of the money in your 401(k) or IRA will be yours to keep in retirement?
a. Most, but not all of it, as I'll owe taxes on money I withdraw.
b. Everything I've invested on an after-tax basis into a Roth IRA or Roth 401(k) is mine, as long as some minimum requirements are met.
c. What do you mean, all of it isn't mine? It's my money, damnit.

Which of the following types of insurance coverage do I currently have or might consider for future needs?
a. Term life insurance, a relatively less expensive coverage that pays a death benefit to beneficiaries only for a designated time period.
b. Permanent life insurance, such as whole life or the different variations of universal life, that pays a death benefit for as long as the policy is funded.
c. Permanent insurance as a tax-favored investment alternative.
d. Long-term care insurance, which provides money to pay for custodial care should I no longer be able to care for myself.
e. Insurance? Listen, my beneficiaries don't need any help from me.

What do you now know about health care coverage for seniors?

a. Medicare covers a lot beginning at age sixty-five, but it doesn't cover everything.

b. "Traditional" Medicare consists of Part A (hospital coverage) and Part B (medical costs such as doctor bills and diagnostic exams). Part D is prescription drug coverage and incurs an additional charge.

c. Medicare supplemental insurance, a.k.a. "Medigap coverage," is offered by private insurance companies to cover the often-costly expenses that traditional Medicare doesn't cover.

d. How can Medicare not cover everything? Didn't I pay taxes for it all my life?

How do you propose to cover your possible long-term care costs should you or a spouse become unable to provide your own care?

a. I will explore traditional long-term care insurance.

b. I will explore long-term care riders that can be added to life insurance or annuity contracts.

c. I will explore setting aside assets to self-fund such expenses.

d. I'm good. My kids will take care of me.

How can I be sure that my spouse and I will receive steady income in retirement and won't outlive our assets?

a. If either of you has a pension, structure its payouts so that they cover the lives of both spouses.

b. Create your own pension-like income streams that are guaranteed for life, such as those provided by insurance products.

c. Develop a long-term income plan that projects living expenses, adjusts annually for inflation, and provides income to meet these expenses.

d. Invest and grow assets that can plug any "income gap" between estimated lifestyle expenses and anticipated "fixed income."

e. We'll be fine; I've always done well in the market. I know a guy who knows a guy.

The next time I even think about estate planning, I will be sure to:
a. Update the beneficiaries on my life insurance policies, bank accounts, and investment accounts.

b. Make an appointment to visit an estate attorney to draw up a will or, better still, a trust.

c. Assign powers of attorney for both medical and everyday business matters to people I trust to make decisions for me should I become incapable of making them myself.

d. None of the above. Frankly, I don't care what happens to my stuff when I'm gone.

How can I be sure I'm actually in position to turn in my retirement notice?
a. I've explored all my Social Security options and fully understand which is best for my situation.

b. I've worked with a financial advisor to develop a comprehensive lifetime income plan that balances my projected living expenses with income I know will be there.

c. I've explored my options for health care in retirement. I now understand better how Medicare and Medigap coverage works.

d. I've worked with an advisor to set up a plan for funding any future long-term care costs that might arise.

e. I've planned a bank heist that should produce enough loot to live on comfortably in Costa Rica.

As you might guess, there is no scoring here, mainly because there is no one correct answer to every question. (We would respectfully suggest, however, that if you selected the final response on each, you likely need more help than we can provide.)

And don't worry if you can't answer everything. Many retirement-related issues are ones you likely haven't had to deal with yet. There is an adage that says, "We often don't know what we don't know," and that's certainly the case with retirement situations.

The good news is, there are people ready and eager to help you become familiar with what you will soon need to know.

Let's take a closer look at two of those people, those whose thoughts and financial philosophies you've been discovering over the course of the previous chapters.

We're Pleased to Meet You

From Aviva Sapers, President and CEO: I always wanted to be in a business where I could help people, be my own boss, and make a decent living. When I thought about doing so, I immediately thought of my dad, Bill Sapers, who represents the second generation of the company that eventually became Sapers & Wallack. Dad always seemed to enjoy what he did in helping people, and that also appealed to me. As I asked more questions about his business and whether he thought I could try it, he beamed from ear to ear. I knew then I was on a good track.

I am very proud of our work helping clients realize financial independence, as well as our work with several Boston-area and national charitable organizations to help them raise more money and spend dollars more wisely.

From Andrew MacDougall, Director of Wealth Management: For as long as I can remember, I always wanted to be in a career that involved finances. I seemed even as a kid to enjoy following stocks, watching them grow, and talking about different financial planning techniques.

My interest became well enough known that in college, some of my friends would approach me with questions about their money matters and ask what I might do if in their shoes. Later, when pursuing my MBA at the D'Amore-McKim School of Business at Northeastern University, their questions turned more to "Should I opt into my company's 401(k)?" or, "Should I take a thirty-year mortgage or fifteen-year?" It eventually occurred to me that I enjoyed talking about these things and how fun it would be to do this all day every day. I couldn't be happier about the decision I made.

A Call to Action

Consider the above quiz, as well as this entire book, a call to action. It's our hope that you will use some of the information in this book to revisit your own financial wellness. Should you have questions or want financial guidance, we invite you to reach out to us.

We will do our best to explain often-complicated issues in a way you can understand. We are happy to address your concerns in matters both big and small. Perhaps it's something as simple—yet important—as changing or updating a beneficiary on an insurance document or investment account. Perhaps it's something involving a major life change: the death of a loved one, a divorce, a career move, or changes you want to make to benefit a new grandchild. Any of these are occasions to review things with a financial advisor or insurance agent.

We all experience changes in life, and enter new phases of our journey. If that new phase is retirement, you have to consider new issues such as: How will I generate regular income now that I no longer earn wages? Where is the best place to pull money from? When should I apply for Social Security? What kind of supplemental health care plan is best for me or a spouse?

You shouldn't have to try to figure all of this out for yourself, and you don't have to. We wrote this book to give you a resource, but working with us can make it even easier for you. You don't have to be the expert. We have the tools. We have the experience. We monitor the markets daily. We know how to explain things in simple-to-understand terms.

You don't have to do this all by yourself. Not when we're here to help.

As noted previously, many of the financial issues we deal with every day can be complicated. Heaven help anyone, for instance, who tries to draw up estate planning documents on their own. This is why you should want an advisor who is familiar with *all* of your financial issues—investments, insurance, health care coverage, tax strategies, estate planning, charitable giving—and can be your first call when you need help.

People of all ages, but especially in retirement years, often tell us it's comforting to know that a surviving spouse can go to one person, a longtime advisor, to find answers when the spouse who handled most of the couple's financial matters is no longer with us. Or, perhaps you just need a little help in filing an insurance claim when someone gets sick or hurt. That's when an advisor who is well-versed in insurance matters can be especially helpful.

Independence is also important in choosing an advisor. One who can bring any product to the table is, in our opinion, in better position to serve your needs than one who is employed by an institution that encourages their agents to push that company's specific products. We are an independent company.

Don't Let Things Slip
Through Your Fingers

If you take nothing else from this book, please take this advice with you.

Don't leave yourself exposed when you could have done the planning necessary to achieve financial independence.

We're going to make an educated guess here and suggest that readers who've read this far into our book have likely done a lot of things right in their lives. We believe you are motivated people, folks who've saved and invested in yourselves and your families and their futures. We also believe that you likely don't know everything you need to know and have come here to learn more about this new phase of life you are about to enter.

Good for you.

You've come a long way in this thing we euphemistically call the game of life, and you know you can't afford to make any losing moves as the "game" nears its late innings. That's why it's now time to **plan to win**.

Just as you wouldn't start a new home construction without a blueprint, neither should you consider entering retirement without a financial plan in place. This should be a plan that tells you exactly how much income will be produced, from where it will come, and how it will keep coming for as long as you need it. This should be a plan that shows you how your health care will be covered. A plan that employs tax strategies to keep as much of your money in your pocket as possible; that provides for future long-term care costs if necessary; that assures that your assets will be passed on in the most efficient manner.

This should be a plan you develop early and update often. Life, after all, is a constant evolution, it throws us curve balls all the time, and your plan should adjust to meet those changes. A trusted advisor can help guide you through this ever-changing environment.

Retirement, we believe, is an opportunity, a chance to do things you once could only dream of doing while you were in the daily workforce.

We have watched first-hand as people go through difficult times financially that could have been avoided. You know how some people don't go to the doctor because they fear being told that something is wrong? Well, the same goes with financial planning. We've seen people making simple mistakes they didn't even realize they were making. And what makes their situation even more sad is that a few small changes, typically ones made with the help of a financial advisor, could have drastically impacted their lives.

Clearly, the key to doing this is advanced planning. If you take away nothing else from this book, please take our advice to prepare for a time that should be yours to enjoy. This will be a period of life in which your time is yours to command. You are about to become your own employer. But that also means you must provide your own paycheck and health insurance, and that requires planning to develop the means to do so.

Don't let this opportunity slip through your fingers. You've worked too hard, come too close to the finish line of your working career. Don't let your hopes and dreams get away from you now because you didn't take the time or effort to plan and prepare for your future. If we can help play a role in your financial success, we would love the opportunity to do so.

Acknowledgments

Aviva Sapers: A special thank you to my father, William Sapers, who not only was my partner for forty years and an icon in our industry but also a tremendous role model and mentor. He taught me to ask questions and to make sure I give back to the community. His constant positive attitude and optimism and his creativity were always inspiring.

I also want to say thank you to our many team members at Sapers & Wallack without whom none of what we do could happen. You know who you are, and I appreciate you. Finally, I would like to thank my wife Jude, who supports me and allows me to spend the time I need doing what I love.

Andrew MacDougall: I'd also like to acknowledge my father, Robert (Bob) MacDougall. He wasn't in the financial services field, but he had a very strong sense of financial knowledge and taught me at a young age to be financially independent. I still remember from my childhood days how he would buy me random stocks for my birthday, and I would watch them fluctuate in value in the Sunday paper.

I'd also like to thank all the mentors and other people who counseled me and provided a sounding board for my many questions while coming up through the ranks of this business. There are too many to name, but I'm thankful for all of them.

About the Authors

AVIVA SAPERS is the president and CEO of Sapers & Wallack. Inc., an employee benefits and financial services company in Newton, Massachusetts. She provides a third generation of leadership in a family business that began in 1932 when her grandfather started as a Sun Life agent and started a company that was eventually joined and expanded by Aviva's father.

During her own forty-year business career, Aviva oversaw the expansion of the insurance agency into a multi-dimensional female-led business that today offers not only insurance, retirement advisory work, and employee and executive benefits, but also wealth management and charitable strategies.

Aviva, who joined her family's company in 1987, became the firm's CEO in 2000. The company was included on the Boston Business Journal's 2008 list of "Area Largest Women-Run Businesses." She is passionate about helping people and has more recently focused on helping women achieve a greater level of financial literacy and independence.

Aviva is a proud mother of two wonderful kids. Active in community and charitable work, she is a member of the Commonwealth Institute and the Boston Estate Planning Council. She also serves on the President's Advisory Council of the Combined Jewish Philanthropies of Greater Boston and the Berklee College of Music. Her love of music—she first began playing the trumpet as a young girl and has sounded the Shofar for over forty years during the high holidays at Temple Israel in Boston—often draws her to concerts and musicals in Boston and has taken her to Italy to the Jazz Festival in Umbria and to Berklee's graduate school in Valencia.

Aviva also is a frequent visitor to Israel, where she takes pride in helping Jews, especially first-time visitors, explore their heritage.

Before joining the family firm, she received her Bachelor's degree from Colby College and an MBA from the Tuck School of Business at Dartmouth. She is an Investment Advisor Representative with degrees as a Certified Life Underwriter (CLU) and a Chartered Financial Consultant (ChFC) from The American College.

ANDREW MacDOUGALL is Director of Wealth Management at Sapers & Wallack, where he brings eighteen years of experience in both the institutional and personal sides of investment management.

Prior to joining Sapers & Wallack, Andrew worked within the Corporate and Investment Bank of JP Morgan. He later served as a managing director-for a Registered Investment Advisor firm in Boston.

Andrew holds a Bachelor's degree from Assumption University and an MBA from Northeastern University. He is a Retirement Income Certified Professional (RICP), Chartered Financial Consultant (CFC), and Certified Financial Planner (CFP).

A father of three, Andrew is an avid sports fan who enjoys playing basketball and golf in his spare time.

End Notes

[1] Liz Weston. nerdwallet.com. March 25, 2021. "Will You Really Run Out of Money in Retirement?" https://www.nerdwallet.com/article/finance/will-you-really-run-out-of-money-in-retirement

[2] Social Security Administration. 2022 Trustees Report. "Actuarial Life Table" https://www.ssa.gov/oact/STATS/table4c6.html

[3] Bob Sullivan, Benjamin Curry. Forbes. April 28, 2021. "Inflation And Retirement Investments: What You Need to Know." https://www.forbes.com/advisor/retirement/inflation-retirement-investments/

[4] Henry J. Kaiser Family Foundation. October 27, 2022. "2022 Employer Health Benefits Survey Section Eleven: Retiree Health Benefits." https://www.kff.org/report-section/ehbs-2022-section-11-retiree-health-benefits/

[5] Fidelity Viewpoints. Fidelity. August 29, 2022.. "How to Plan for Rising Health Care Costs." https://www.fidelity.com/viewpoints/personal-finance/plan-for-rising-health-care-costs

[6] Richard W. Johnson. urban.org. June 24, 2021. "What is the Lifetime Risk of Needing and Receiving Long-Term Services and Supports?" https://www.urban.org/research/publication/what-lifetime-risk-needing-and-receiving-long-term-services-and-supports

[7] Genworth Financial. June 2022. "Cost of Care Survey 2022." https://www.genworth.com/aging-and-you/finances/cost-of-care.html

[8] Medicare.gov. "What Part A covers." https://www.medicare.gov/what-medicare-covers/part-a/what-part-a-covers.html

[9] Medicare.gov. "When can I sign up for Medicare?" https://www.medicare.gov/basics/get-started-with-medicare/sign-up/when-can-i-sign-up-for-medicare

[10] Medicare. "Medicare 2023 Costs at a Glance." https://www.medicare.gov/your-medicare-costs/medicare-costs-at-a-glance

[11] Ibid.

[12] Medicare. "Costs in the coverage gap." https://www.medicare.gov/drug-coverage-part-d/costs-for-medicare-drug-coverage/costs-in-the-coverage-gap

[13] American Association for Long-Term Care Insurance. 2023. "Long-Term Care Insurance Facts – Data – Statistics – 2022 Reports" https://www.aaltci.org/long-term-care-insurance/learning-center/ltcfacts-2022.php#2022costs-65. Note: Figure cited is for the State of Illinois.

[14] payingforseniorcare.com. 2022. "Long-Term Senior Care Statistics" https://www.payingforseniorcare.com/statistics

[15] Genworth Financial. January 31, 2022. "Genworth 2020 Cost of Care Survey." https://www.genworth.com/aging-and-you/finances/cost-of-care.html

[16] Riders are available for an additional fee. Some riders may not be available in all states.

[17] pewtrusts.org. September 14, 2021. "The State Pension Funding Gap: Plans Have Stabilized in Wake of Pandemic" https://www.pewtrusts.org/en/research-and-analysis/issue-briefs/2021/09/the-state-pension-funding-gap-plans-have-stabilized-in-wake-of-pandemic

[18] Amin Dabit. personalcapital.com. April 1, 2021. "The Average 401k Balance by Age." https://www.personalcapital.com/blog/retirement-planning/average-401k-balance-age/

[19] Kamaron McNair. magnifymoney.com. October 26, 2021. "Nearly 30% of Millennials Still Receive Financial Support From Their Parents" https://www.magnifymoney.com/blog/news/parental-financial-support-survey/

[20] tradingeconomics.com. 2022 Data/2023 Forecast/1914-2021 Historical. "United States Inflation Rate" https://tradingeconomics.com/united-states/inflation-cpi

[21] U.S. Inflation Calculator. "United States Core Inflation Rates (1957-2022)" https://www.usinflationcalculator.com/inflation/united-states-core-inflation-rates/

[22] In2013dollars.com. "$2 in 1997 is worth $3.70 today" https://www.in2013dollars.com/us/inflation/1997?amount=2

[23] In2013dollars.com "Admission to movies, theaters, and concerts priced at $20 in 1997>$40.34 in 2022" https://www.in2013dollars.com/Admission-to-movies,-theaters,-and-concerts/price-inflation

[24] Moll Law Group. 2022. "The Cost of Long-Term Care." https://www.molllawgroup.com/the-cost-of-long-term-care.html

[25] Palash Ghosh. Forbes.com. May 6, 2021. "A Third Of Seniors Seek To Work Well Past Retirement Age, Or Won't Retire At All, Poll Finds" https://www.forbes.com/sites/palashghosh/2021/05/06/a-third-of-seniors-seek-to-work-well-past-retirement-age-or-wont-retire-at-all-poll-finds/?sh=1d2ece836b95

[26] Diversification does not guarantee a profit or protect against a loss in a declining market. It is a method use to help manage investment risk.

[27] Risk tolerance is an investor's general ability to withstand the risk inherent in investing. The risk tolerance questionnaire is designed to determine your risk tolerance and is judged based on three factors: time horizon, long-term goals and expectations, and short-term risk attitudes. The adviser uses their own experience and subjective evaluation of your answers to help determine your risk tolerance.
There is no guarantee that the risk assessment questionnaire will accurately assess your tolerance to risk. In addition, although the advisor may have directly or indirectly used the results of this questionnaire to determine a suggested asset allocation, there is no guarantee that the asset mix appropriately reflects your ability to withstand investment risk.

[28] Mutual Funds and Exchange Traded Funds (ETF's) are sold by prospectus. Please consider the investment objectives, risks, charges, and expenses carefully before investing. The prospectus, which contains this and other information about the investment company, can be obtained from the fund.

[29] A REIT is a security that sells like a stock on the major exchanges and invests in real estate directly, either through properties or mortgages. REITs receive special tax considerations and typically offer investors high yields, as well as a highly liquid method of investing in real estate. There are risks associated with these types of investments and include but are not limited to the following: Typically, no secondary market exists for the security listed above. Potential difficulty discerning between routine interest payments and principal repayment. Redemption price of a REIT may be worth more or less than the original price paid. Value of the shares in the trust will fluctuate with the portfolio of underlying real estate. Involves risks such as refinancing in the real estate industry, interest rates, availability of mortgage funds, operating expenses, cost of insurance, lease terminations, potential economic and regulatory changes. This is neither an offer to sell nor a solicitation or an offer to buy the securities described herein. The offering is made only by the Prospectus.

[30] Investing in alternative assets involves higher risks than traditional investments and is suitable only for sophisticated investors. Alternative investments are often sold by prospectus that discloses all risks, fees, and expenses. They are not tax efficient and an investor should consult with his/her tax advisor prior to investing. Alternative investments have higher fees than traditional investments and they may also be highly leveraged and engage in speculative investment techniques, which can magnify the potential for investment loss or gain and should not be deemed a complete investment program. The value of the investment may fall as well as rise and investors may get back less than they invested.

[31] Any references to protection or steady and reliable income streams refer only to fixed insurance products. They do not refer, in any way, to securities or investment advisory products.

[32] Asset Allocation does not guarantee a profit or protect against a loss in a declining market. It is a method used to help manage investment risk.

[33] Private placements are high risk and illiquid investments. As with other investments, you can lose some or all of your investment. Nothing here should be interpreted to state or imply that past results are an indication of future performance nor should it be interpreted that FINRA, the SEC or any other securities regulator approves of any of these

securities. Additionally, there are no warranties expressed or implied as to accuracy, completeness, or results obtained any information provided here. Investing in private securities transactions bears risk, in part due to the following factors: there is no secondary market for the securities; there is credit risk; where there is collateral as security for the investment, its value may be impaired if it is sold. Please see the Private Placement Memorandum (PPM) for a more detailed explanation of expenses and risks.

[34] Pam Krueger. Kiplinger.com. January 8, 2021. "How to Spot (and Squash) Nasty Fees That Hide in Your Investments" https://www.kiplinger.com/retirement/retirement-planning/602043/how-to-spot-and-squash-nasty-fees-that-hide-in-your

[35] Dollar cost averaging may help reduce per share cost through continuous investment in securities regardless of fluctuating prices and does not guarantee profitability nor can it protect from loss in a declining market. The investor should consider his/her ability to continue investing through periods of low-price levels.

[36] Indices are unmanaged and investors cannot invest directly in an index. Unless otherwise noted, performance of indices does not account for any fees, commissions or other expenses that would be incurred. Returns do not include reinvested dividends. The Standard & Poor's 500 (S&P 500) Index is a free-float weighted index that tracks the 500 most widely held stocks on the NYSE or NASDAQ and is representative of the stock market in general. It is a market value weighted index with each stock's weight in the index proportionate to its market value.

[37] Returns reflect price index only and do not include dividends. Intra-year drops reflect the largest market drop from peak to trough during the calendar year. Source: FactSet; Standard & Poor's; JP Morgan Asset Management

[38] Please consider the investment objectives, risks, charges, and expenses carefully before investing in Variable Annuities. The prospectus, which contains this and other information about the variable annuity contract and the underlying investment options, can be obtained from the insurance company or your financial professional. Be sure to read the prospectus carefully before deciding whether to invest.
The investment return and principal value of the variable annuity investment options are not guaranteed. Variable annuity sub-accounts fluctuate with changes in market conditions. The principal may be worth more or less than the original amount invested when the annuity is surrendered.

[39] Fixed annuities are long-term insurance contacts and there is a surrender charge imposed generally during the first 5 to 7 years that you own the annuity contract. Withdrawals prior to age 59-1/2 may result in a 10% IRS tax penalty, in addition to any ordinary income tax. Any guarantees of the annuity are backed by the financial strength of the underlying insurance company.

[40] Indexed annuities are insurance contracts that, depending on the contract, may offer a guaranteed annual interest rate and some participation growth, if any, of a stock market index. Such contracts have substantial variation in terms, costs of guarantees and features and may cap participation or returns in significant ways. Any guarantees offered are backed by the financial strength of the insurance company. Surrender charges apply if not held to the end of the term. Withdrawals are taxed as ordinary income and, if taken prior to 59 ½, a 10% federal tax penalty. Investors are cautioned to carefully review an indexed annuity for its features, costs, risks, and how the variables are calculated.

[41] With variable annuities, the money you invest in sub-accounts resides directly with the investment companies that manage the mutual funds within those accounts. As a result, even if the insurance company writing the annuity contract goes out of business, your money is still protected by the financial stability of the investment companies that manage the funds in the sub-accounts.

[42] The above opinion is not associated with or endorsed by the Social Security Administration or any other government agency.

[43] ssa.gov. "Alternate Measure of Replacement Rates for Social Security Benefits and Retirement Income" https://www.ssa.gov/policy/docs/ssb/v68n2/v68n2p1.html.

[44] Chris Kissell. moneytalknews.com. January 20, 2021. "This Is When the Most People Start Taking Social Security." https://www.moneytalksnews.com/the-most-popular-age-for-claiming-social-security/

[45] Social Security Administration. "Full Retirement Age." https://www.ssa.gov/planners/retire/retirechart.html

[46] Social Security Administration. April 2021. "Can You Take Your Benefits Before Full Retirement Age?" https://www.ssa.gov/planners/retire/applying2.html

[47] Social Security Administration. "Cost-Of-Living Adjustment (COLA) Information for 2022." https://www.ssa.gov/cola/

[48] Social Security Administration. "Retirement Planner: Benefits For You As A Spouse." https://www.ssa.gov/planners/retire/applying6.html

[49] Office of the Chief Actuary. Social Security Administration. "Social Security Benefits: Benefits for Spouses." https://www.ssa.gov/OACT/quickcalc/spouse.html#calculator

[50] Social Security Administration. "Retirement Planner: If You Are Divorced." https://www.ssa.gov/planners/retire/divspouse.html

[51] Social Security Administration. "Social Security Benefit Amounts For The Surviving Spouse By Year Of Birth." https://www.ssa.gov/planners/survivors/survivorchartred.html

[52] Social Security Administration. "Benefits Planner: Income Taxes and Your Social Security Benefits." https://www.ssa.gov/planners/taxes.html

[53] Social Security Administration. "Receiving Benefits White Working" https://www.ssa.gov/benefits/retirement/planner/whileworking.html.

[54] usdebtclock.org.

[55] Jim Probasco. Investopedia.com. January 6, 2023. "SECURE 2.0 Act of 2022." https://www.investopedia.com/secure-2-0-definition-5225115

[56] Bureau of Labor Statistics. September 22, 2020. "Employee Tenure Summary." https://www.bls.gov/news.release/tenure.nr0.htm

[57] Investment Company Institute. October 11, 2021. "Frequently Asked Questions About 401(k) Plan Research" https://www.ici.org/faqs/faq/401k/faqs_401k#:~:text=In%202020%2C%20there%20were%20about,of%20former%20employees%20and%20retirees.

[58] IRS.gov. December 8, 2022. "401(k) limit increases to $22,500 for 2023, IRA limit rises to $6,500" https://www.irs.gov/newsroom/401k-limit-increases-to-22500-for-2023-ira-limit-rises-to-6500

[59] Fidelity.com. 2023. "SECURE 2.0: Rethinking retirement savings" https://www.fidelity.com/learning-center/personal-finance/secure-act-2

[60] Ibid.

[61] Betterment.com. January 12, 2023. "SECURE Act 2.0: Signed into Law" https://www.betterment.com/work/resources/secure-act-2

[62] Bob Carlson. Forbes. January 28, 2020. "More Questions And Answers About The SECURE Act." https://www.forbes.com/sites/bobcarlson/2020/01/28/more-questions-and-answers-about-the-secure-act/#113d49564869

[63] Converting an employer plan account or Traditional IRA to a Roth IRA is a taxable event. Increased taxable income from the Roth IRA conversion may have several consequences including but not limited to, a need for additional tax withholding or estimated tax payments, the loss of certain tax deductions and credits, and higher taxes on Social Security benefits and higher Medicare premiums. Be sure to consult with a qualified tax advisor before making any decisions regarding your IRA.

[64] Greg Greenburg, Investment News, June 22, 2023. "Americans say they need $1.27 million to retire comfortably, survey shows." https://www.investmentnews.com/americans-say-they-need-1-27-million-to-retire-comfortably-survey-shows-238992

[65] Lindsay Modglin. singlecare.com. February 15, 2022. "Long-term care statistics 2022. https://www.singlecare.com/blog/news/long-term-care-statistics/

[66] American Association for Long-Term Care Insurance. 2023. "Nearly Half Of Oldest Long-Term Care Insurance Applicants Denied" https://www.aaltci.org/news/long-term-care-insurance-association-news/applicants-declined e

[67] aaltci.org. 2023. "2022 Price Index For Long-Term Care Insurance Released" https://www.aaltci.org/news/long-term-care-insurance-association-news/2022-price-index-for-long-term-care-insurance

[68] thezebra.com. January 31, 2023. "House Fire Statistics". https://www.thezebra.com/resources/research/house-fire-statistics/

[69] Erin Duffin. Statista. December 12, 2022. "Number of households in the U.S. from 1960 to 2022" https://www.statista.com/statistics/183635/number-of-households-in-the-us/

[70] hcgsecure.com. 2022. "Long-Term Care Perceptions & Preparation" https://hcgsecure.com/independent-research/

[71] American Association for Long-Term Care Insurance. 2022. "Long Term Care Insurance Partnership Plans." http://www.aaltci.org/long-term-care-insurance/learning-center/long-term-care-insurance-partnership-plans.php

[72] American Council On Aging. March 14, 2022. "How Purchasing Long-Term Care Insurance Can Help Medicaid Beneficiaries Protect Their Homes & Assets" https://www.medicaidplanningassistance.org/partnerships-for-long-term-care/

[73] Genworth. November 16, 2021. "Beyond Dollars 2021." chrome-extension://efaidnbmnnnibpcajpcglclefindmkaj/https://pro.genworth.com/riiproweb/productinfo/pdf/682801BRO.pdf

[74] IRS.gov. December 20, 2022. "What's New — Estate and Gift Tax" https://www.irs.gov/businesses/small-businesses-self-employed/whats-new-estate-and-gift-tax

[75] Administration for Community Living. November 30, 2022. "Profile of Older Americans." https://acl.gov/aging-and-disability-in-america/data-and-research/profile-older-americans

[76] Social Security Administration. "Retirement Planner: Benefits For You As A Spouse." https://www.ssa.gov/planners/retire/applying6.html

[77] Social Security Administration. "Retirement Planner: If You Are Divorced." https://www.ssa.gov/planners/retire/divspouse.html

[78] Social Security Administration. "Survivors Planner: If You Are The Worker's Widow Or Widower." https://www.ssa.gov/planners/survivors/ifyou.html#h2

[79] Martin Armstrong. World Economic Forum. April 29, 2022. "How old are the world's oldest people?" https://www.weforum.org/agenda/2022/04/the-oldest-people-in-the-world/

[80] Megan Leonhardt. cnbc.com. June 16, 2021. "58% of men were able to continue saving for retirement during the pandemic—but only 41% of women were." https://www.cnbc.com/2021/06/16/why-pandemic-hit-womens-retirement-savings-more-than-mens.html

[81] Lindsay Modglin. singlecare.com. February 15, 2022. "Long-term care statistics 2022" https://www.singlecare.com/blog/news/long-term-care-statistics/

[82] statistica.com. November 23, 2022. "Share of senior households living alone in the United States 2020, by gender" https://www.statista.com/statistics/912400/senior-households-living-alone-usa/

[83] caregiving.org. 2020 Report. "Caregiving in the U.S. 2020." https://www.caregiving.org/caregiving-in-the-us-2020/

[84] Nancy Kerr. AARP. June 29, 2021. " Family Caregivers Spend More Than $7,200 a Year on Out-of-Pocket Costs." https://www.aarp.org/caregiving/financial-legal/info-2021/high-out-of-pocket-costs.html

[85] Maurie Backman. The Motley Fool. March 4, 2021. "A Summary of 20 Years of Research and Statistics on Women in Investing." https://www.fool.com/research/women-in-investing-research/

[86] "Volunteering and Its Surprising Benefits." https://www.helpguide.org/articles/healthy-living/volunteering-and-its-surprising-benefits.htm

[87] Dawn Papandrea. Lendingtree. November 29, 2021. "56% of Americans Donated to Charity in 2021, at Average of $574." https://www.lendingtree.com/debt-consolidation/charitable-donations-survey-study/

[88] IRS.gov. August 25, 2022. "Charitable Contribution Deductions" https://www.irs.gov/charities-non-profits/charitable-organizations/charitable-contribution-deductions#.

[89] Council on Foundations. 2022. "IRA Charitable Rollover" https://www.cof.org/content/ira-charitable-rollover-0#

MADE IN USA

Made in the USA
Middletown, DE
12 November 2023

42487449R00104